Timothy Dwight

Thoughts of and for the inner life

Sermons

Timothy Dwight

Thoughts of and for the inner life
Sermons

ISBN/EAN: 9783337160050

Printed in Europe, USA, Canada, Australia, Japan

Cover: Foto ©Lupo / pixelio.de

More available books at **www.hansebooks.com**

SERMONS

BY

TIMOTHY DWIGHT

PRESIDENT OF YALE UNIVERSITY

The kingdom of God is within you

NEW YORK
DODD, MEAD AND COMPANY
1899

TO

The Brotherhood of Yale University,

Graduates and Undergraduates.

I DEDICATE THIS VOLUME

AS A TESTIMONIAL OF MY KINDLY FRIENDSHIP FOR
THEM, AND OF MY INTEREST IN THEIR
HIGHEST WELFARE.

PREFACE.

THE thoughts expressed in these sermons are, in accordance with the title which is given to the volume, thoughts of and for the inner life. Such sermons are perhaps less often presented to hearers and readers in these now passing years than those which deal with external work and service and with the great activities of the Church on behalf of men who are outside of its limits. The inner life, however, does not lose its interest, or its infinite worth, to the Christian mind. The author hopes that some thoughtful Christians may find in what he has written a measure of useful suggestion that may repay them for the time which they chance to spend in looking over the pages of the volume. Thoughts are among the richest blessings which come to us in this world. Thoughts of the inner life are often richer than those of the outer life.

The idea of the Christian life, which, in large measure at least, underlies the suggestions of the sermons, is that of a personal fellowship, a Divine-human friendship, if we may use the term, between the believer and Christ. This is the Johannean idea, as set before us in the Fourth Gospel and the First Epistle, and is, to the mind of the writer of these discourses, one of the most beautiful and inspiring of all the thoughts presented to us in the New Testament.

The sermons have, most of them, been preached in the Chapel of Yale University to the audiences assembled there from time to time. Two or three of them have within themselves, as they are now printed, the evidences, very strongly marked, of their special purpose in relation to a company of young College men. Two or three others bear in them indications that they were written with reference to persons in a different sphere of life, or of a more advanced age. These things, however, are merely incidental, and, it is believed, will in no case lessen the interest or helpfulness — if, indeed, there be anything of this character pertaining to them — which they may have for any reader.

The volume now goes forth whithersoever it will — or whithersoever it may. May it bear a message of peace and of love in itself.

TIMOTHY DWIGHT.

Yale University, April, 1899.

CONTENTS.

I

THE UNNAMED DISCIPLE

One of the two that heard John speak, and followed Jesus, was Andrew, Simon Peter's brother. — JOHN i. 40.

THE words of this verse form a part of a brief story from which as a centre or starting-point the entire Gospel which the Church ascribes to the Apostle John moves toward the fulfilment of its purpose. The story tells of two disciples of John the Baptist, who were pointed by him to Jesus as the Son of God. They followed Jesus, and at His invitation spent two hours with Him at the place of His temporary sojourning. In that brief interview they heard and saw enough to strengthen in their minds the conviction that He was, indeed, what the prophet-teacher had testified concerning Him, and at its close they returned to their own lodgings. This is all that the narrative relates; but the writer adds the statement, that one of the two was Andrew, Simon Peter's brother. Of the other he says nothing which may determine his personality. What does the verse, as thus connected with the story, — what does the story, as we think of the two young men, suggest to us?

It is certainly interesting to notice, that, so far as the Gospels give us any account of the ministry of

Jesus, these two young men were the first ones who became His disciples. As that Jewish day closed at six o'clock in the evening, and their two hours' conversation came to its end, they constituted the company of believers — the Christian Church. What was their personal condition? How much did they know? We cannot suppose that they had made any considerable progress in the understanding of the great spiritual truths which Jesus had come to reveal. It was long after this that they were so undeveloped and uncomprehending as to awaken His astonishment at their slowness of heart to believe. It was even at the very latest hour of His life with them, that they continued to cherish the thought of a temporal kingdom, and were filled not only with sorrow, but with wonder and disappointment of their hopes, when His departure from them to the heavenly world was revealed as a thing of the immediate and certain future. They could have heard but little from Him in those short hours — only enough to give them some impression of His personality and some passing glimpse into the depths of His inner life. But they certainly saw for themselves — this the narrative makes abundantly clear to us — that which caused the declaration of John the Baptist to become a living reality to their own consciousness. He had said to them, the day before, that a certain sign had been made known to him, and that he had been told that, when that sign should be manifested with reference to one among the number of those who were coming to him for his baptism, he could recognise by means of it the

Messiah, to prepare whose way was his appointed
mission; — and he had added the statement that,
after a time, he had seen the sign appear as this
man was baptised. The interview with Jesus had
led them to believe that John was right, and that the
Divine Spirit was with this extraordinary man.
But this was probably the sum of the impression
produced upon them. What the wonderful power
was which lay within His mind and heart, they
probably did not appreciate in any measure; nor
did they know, if they put themselves under His
guidance, to what He would lead them. We may
believe, also, that the faith which they had was not
secure against all dangers of the future. They could
scarcely, in those two hours, have gained a foundation for their living, in whose security they could
themselves have had entire confidence. They had,
however, made a beginning, and it was a peaceful one for their hearts. There are some things
very instructive in their progress from that hour
onwards.

One of these is, that they came to Jesus again,
the next day, and sought to learn more of what He
might have to tell them. They went with Him to
Cana, where they saw the great miracle — perhaps
to Jerusalem, where He first entered publicly upon
His office. They suffered themselves to be won by
His words and teachings, and to open their hearts to
receive more and more. They did not give way to
doubts or questionings which might naturally have
arisen, but seeing in Him from the outset a helpful

3

friend, they trusted and waited. A little while afterwards, they joined Him for their life's work, and
lived in His society. They entered more and more
fully into His living, and tried more and more completely to transfer the secret of that living to their
own souls. They found, as they moved onward, that
life became richer and deeper, broader and more
far-reaching, as they did this. In a wonderful way,
they discovered themselves to be ready to give up
all things for His sake. Still more wonderfully —
when the years had passed and, with them, He had
gone into the unseen — they learned that, in His
absence, He was nearer and more to them than He
had been even in His personal presence. As they
looked back from the time near the end of their
earthly career, they saw that the progress had been
unbroken and uninterrupted, and they believed, as
sincerely as men ever believe anything — they knew,
with as much confidence as men ever know anything
— that they had made no mistake in following the
impulses of that hour of their early manhood. And
then they died, in a calm, sweet, joyful hope of something better — of a reunion with the Friend whom
they had learned to love, and of being like Him
when they should see Him again.

Another thing is, that the two — so far as we get
any knowledge of them from the Gospels and in
their subsequent career — were very different men.
Andrew seems, probably, to have been a solid,
earnest, yet ordinary character; a man to be trusted
and respected, but not prominent like his brother,

Simon Peter. He was one of the two. The other was the writer of the Fourth Gospel and the one who tells this opening story. The Christian Church, in all the ages, has supposed him to be the Apostle John. But he gives himself no name. The book, however, reveals to us much of what he was and brings us into a knowledge of his inner life. He was, evidently, a man who dwelt largely in the region of that inner life. He was contemplative, introvertive, rich and deep in his thoughts; finding his delight in his own meditations; watchful of the workings of truth in his individual character; with a singular capacity for a pure friendship; having deep emotions; fitted to teach the lessons of holy love; able to realise in himself, more than most men, the highest ideal of the soul. He was worthy to be the disciple whom Jesus loved.

But, notwithstanding the wide difference, what they began to learn at that first meeting with Jesus accomplished the same result for the two. It became the origin of and starting-point for the peculiar growth of character which they knew in their experience afterwards. It showed the same marvellous power to work along the lines of Andrew's life, which it manifested in the life of his companion. It gradually made him more earnest, more trustworthy, more devoted to good works, more ready to live for others, more confident that life belongs to the future rather than the present. If he had anything of Peter's character and Peter's experience, — if he resembled, even though with less of the same qualities, his brother, as he may well have done, — he

5

found his earnestness and his impulses coming constantly under the controlling influences of a new power, and his life glorified by an ennobling principle. What it did for his associate the following narrative tells too plainly, and the world knows too well, to require it to be set forth anew. But it moved in the region of his emotions, his impulses, his love, his thoughtfulness, his rich, calm living, as if it were adapted only to natures like his. It took hold upon the ardor of his fiery passions, which would, at the first, have called down fire from heaven upon those who refused his message, and made the latest and often-repeated exhortation of his closing years, which he addressed to every Christian believer within his influence, to be in the words, Little children, love one another. It penetrated within the ambitious feeling of the earlier manhood, whose desire and demand were for the highest places in the new kingdom, and, by its gradual yet silent energy, so transformed it into a loftier sentiment that, half a century afterward, he was not willing even to name himself in his own writing. He was gladly ready to leave the world without the knowledge of the author of the beautiful story which he had to tell, if so be that it would only believe in Him of whose kingdom and power and love the story was designed to be full.

We can think of the two, at the end, and so of Peter and James, of Nathanael and Philip, who came to Jesus immediately afterward, as each one of them feeling in his own soul and saying to himself, that the energising force gained on that first day, which had wrought such a change in character as the years moved on, could have been fitted for no other life so perfectly as for his own, — and wondering, as we sometimes do when we are thinking, in the joy of our own experience, of the best and truest things of life, such as friendship, love, and home, whether they can be to any other what they are to us. But that they are to every one what they are to us — only with a richer gift as the nature, which is open to receive it, is richer and deeper — is the very proof that they are the truest and best things in our living. And so that friendship with Jesus was the most real of all things to each one of that company while they lived, and when they died.

Another thing, which we may notice, is, that the confidence of the two men in the reality of the friendship and its life-giving force was the same, and that all their life's progress, so far as their belief in what Jesus taught them was concerned, was a very quiet and restful one. They had stormy conflicts in their lives, as all men have; as all men engaged in a good cause in such an age most peculiarly must have had. They were exposed to the doubtings and opposition of enemies to their faith. They may, moreover, have seen many difficulties in the system of doctrine to which they were committed, whose full solution must be waited for until some coming time or clearer day. They certainly had a terrible trial of their belief when they saw all the old ideas derived from their early education overthrown by the crucifixion of the Messiah. They may, no

7

doubt, have been despondent; and have questioned the reality of their own belief or love sometimes. But it is manifest that, when they retired in thought into that central place in their minds where their faith in Christ and His teaching dwelt, they were perfectly peaceful. Whether their faith was weaker or stronger; whether it was as at the first hour, or at the last; it was *in itself* calm and conscious of its own foundation. They did not have to argue for it with themselves, or strengthen it by contending against other systems of belief, or spend their time, on their own behalf, in supporting it and undertaking laborious defences of it, or encourage their hearts against the dangers of its possible failure by making a continual outcry about it of any sort. So far as it existed in their hearts, the wonderful fact about it was, that it was something *for them to rest upon,* — and not something which needed, *for itself, to lean upon them* — their confidence, their arguments, or even their willingness to keep it alive within themselves. It was wonderfully like the truth, in this regard. It seemed to be wonderfully near to the truth.

This was the fact, also, with the whole Apostolic company in the subsequent years. The argumentative writer of the Pauline Epistles, who seems as if eager for conflict with any and every enemy, who moves along the defences of the Christian system as if the hero of a hundred battles, and tries everywhere to subdue the assailant and strengthen the courage of the doubting by appealing to proofs and evidences; and, on the other hand, the medi-

tative author of the Gospel narrative, who tells
a simple story of what he saw in earlier years,
and leaves the strange facts and the deep thoughts
to make their own impression, are alike, when they
come to their individual faith. They are not
afraid of discussions with other men when necessity
arises, but they do not live on them or in them
within themselves. Different from each other as
they may be in every other regard, they are at one
here. And so are all the rest, Andrew and Peter,
Philip and his friend Nathanael, James the Lord's
brother and James the son of Zebedee, each and
all find something, as they first meet the Lord,
which becomes to their souls, and remains ever in
their souls, a firm foundation of character and of
hope — which bears in itself, for the personal life,
the gift of a calm and peaceful joy, when it makes
its first entrance into that life, and which knows
no fears for its own safety or dangers for its own
permanence ever afterward.

We may notice again, that the effect of the meeting
with Jesus upon the action of the two men was the
same. The narrative distinctly states, with respect
to one of them, that he went immediately to his
brother, and made known to him what he believed
himself to have found. It indicates — what is more
clear to the reader of the original than it can be in
our English Version — that the other did the same
thing. With the impulse which comes to every
generous, manly man, to give to another the knowledge of what has proved a great blessing in his

own experience, they told their story to these members of their households. Apparently, from the
records of the other Gospels, these two pairs of
brothers and their families had been previously in
the relations of friendship. We cannot wonder,
therefore, that the two who had the first opportunity
of a conversation with the man to whom John the
Baptist had pointed them, and who had been so
impressed by His personality and His words, should
have desired to bring the other two to meet Him
and to hear Him. Philip did the same thing for
Nathanael.

How naturally it was done! How quietly, and
away from the knowledge of the rulers and the
world! How far from the dreamings even of the
Jewish authorities, or the Pharisees and the scribes,
was the thought that a new power had begun to
work in the world on that afternoon. But the next
morning there were six disciples, where there had
been before none at all; and the number was
never to be so small as on that second morning,
for eighteen hundred years. It was, on the other
hand, to grow and enlarge — until, after a season,
the Jewish authorities were to pass away — and,
after a longer period, the new power was to lay
hold upon governments and nations — and, when
centuries had elapsed, was to become the mightiest
force in the world. But the growth was to be constantly in the same way. The one man — or each
one of the two men, if so it has chanced to be —
discovers the power for himself and in his own life.
He comes, by some means, into communication

with Jesus Christ, into His society, under His influence. He gains what each of those men gained
on that afternoon, and he tells the story of his own
happiness to his friend. Who shall know it? Who
can prevent it? But the secret of the power is
there.

The Church began its history in the hours of
that first meeting. It took to itself in those first
hours, and in the hours that followed after them,
its Divinely given life and its ever-living forces.
By reason of these forces it put forth its power, as
the very necessity of the life to which they belonged
— a power which moved, like the forces of nature,
quietly but resistlessly — and the great work went
onward as with a Divine energy. The beginning,
we may well remember, was with the two men and
the one man, and in their coming together. The
first movement forward was with the two men and
their brothers, and in the words which were spoken.
The progress of the history has been like the
beginning.

Once more we may notice, that the two persons
in the story were, in a special sense, unknown men.
Not only were they obscure Galilean fishermen,
away from the centres of life and influence. Even
so far as the history presents them to us, they were
out of the world's view. One of them appears in
the Gospel narrative only in three or four places,
and of his life we have but little information, either
then or afterwards. The other withdraws himself
almost wholly from sight, and is the unnamed dis-

ciple. IIis personality becomes known to us only by testimony from others, and by inferences which we draw from what he says. Their inspiration sprang from sources hidden, as far as possible, from the notice of mankind. They doubtless thought of themselves, that afternoon, as quite insignificant persons, who had little chance or hope of wide influence. They had been attracted by the power of John the Baptist's preaching, and had been aroused to new and deeper views of life through what he said. They now came to Jesus, because of what John had told them, that they might discover some good for themselves — perhaps, without a thought or expectation of ever talking with Him again — almost certainly without the idea of becoming preachers of His truth and doctrine. But in those two hours they received the beginning of a new life, and a strange impulse to speak of it to their friends. They began immediately the work of building up the Church in the world. Half-unconscious they were, no doubt, of what they were doing. But they were doing; — obscure men, as they were, setting in motion forces which would never cease.

What an impressive scene, that on which our thoughts are turning is, as we think of it thus. One of the two that heard John speak and followed Jesus was Andrew, Simon Peter's brother. Andrew was only Simon Peter's brother — and nothing in himself. And he was one of the two. Who was the other, we ask instinctively, as we read the words. With how much deeper interest — with an interest and wonder how continually increasing and deepening — does the question repeat itself, as we read on through the chapters and see what a man he was. But the only answer is, He was the disciple whom Jesus loved. He follows along the pathway of the Master's life. He goes with Him in the bright hours, and the dark hours. He finds his place next Him at the last supper. He is with Him in the garden, at His examination in the house of Annas, and at the cross. He is the one for whom the longest life and work seem to be appointed. But he never tells us his name, or fully answers our question. He moves our souls, and testifies for the Lord, not by his position or the honours bestowed upon him; but simply by the story which he has to relate, and the evident transforming and uplifting power of the things recorded in the story upon his own character. The unnamed disciple has had more elevating influence for the noblest minds and hearts, by the incidental manifestations of what he was and what Christianity did for him, than any other man, perhaps, that has ever lived.

I know of no little narrative in all the Gospel story, which has more of suggestion in it than this one whose closing words are in our text. And especially are the suggestions those which encourage confidence in our Christian faith.

As we look along the line of our own experience, how remarkable it is, that, while sceptics and doubters all about us are always discussing and questioning — never themselves at rest, and never suffering those who disagree with them, and believe

the Christian truth, to be in the undisturbed possession of their faith, — every Christian believer
finds peaceful quiet in himself so soon as he accepts
the Christian teaching; that he does not find himself compelled to prop his faith by constant arguments, or to strengthen it by showing his enemy's
weakness; that he lets it *take care of itself*, and feels
sure that it will *take care of him ;* that he has the
same sense of restfulness in it, when he is seventy,
as when he is thirty; that this is so in men of all
characters, and all ages, and all differences, so soon
as the faith comes to them, and they are near to
Christ. I think that the things which we can leave
thus in our souls, without supposing them to be in
danger unless we are always contending for them in
ourselves or with others — which every man who has
them is disposed thus to leave, because they seem
to him, at once and always, to have a firm foundation — bear with them, in this very fact, the strongest
evidence that they are thus founded. The doubters
do not rest quietly in their doubts, and the mind
never does in negations.

And then, what a wonderful thing is influence.
It seemed but an accident that Jesus happened to be
passing in the neighbourhood of John the Baptist on
that afternoon, and that those two young men had
the opportunity of meeting Him for an hour or two.
But there went forth from His words and His presence a force which took hold upon them both.
The force moved them both to action, as has been
already said. In the case of the one, we have no

record of the later years, but we know that his new
influence began at once in the persuasion of his
brother, and we know that it went out everywhere,
wherever that brother carried the Gospel message, as
well as wherever he carried it himself. And thus it
reached beyond his knowledge of its limits, as well
as beyond our knowledge. The other of the two,
long years afterwards, when his associates of the
Apostolic company had passed away and life was
advancing far onward towards its ending for himself,
was moved — perhaps by the discussions of cultivated men around him in the city where he lived,
respecting God and His connection with the world
— to tell of his own life with Jesus. With no desire
to speak of himself, except as showing that he had
seen and heard the things which he relates, and thus
giving weight to his testimony, he presents much of
the record of his own history and of the explanation as to how his life came to be what it was. The
little book goes out to those for whom it was intended, and, by accident or Providence as we say, it
is preserved for the future. It goes hither and
thither, — and down the generations. A few years
ago, it opened its power in my soul, or yours. The
world put on a new aspect to our view, and seemed
under a heavenly influence all at once. Life grew
to us less external, and more internal. The Friend,
whom he met so long ago, appeared as a real presence to our thought. He spoke to us by His Spirit,
as He did with the voice to this writer and his
associate. New impulses came to us; new faith was
awakened; deeper life began. The old question-

ings passed away, and peacefulness followed. And
we tell the story of it all to those whom we love most
tenderly, as the best thing which we can give them
in life, and for life. One of the two was Andrew.
Who was the other? He was a man in the ages
long since passed away, who had a beautiful life in a
beautiful soul, and it was gained in Christ's presence
from Christ's teaching. It was the thought that
worked in his mind and heart, which constituted the
peculiar influence — and it matters little who he
was, or who we are. The greatest of Heaven's gifts
to us may be just this — that the influence came
forth from him and reached to our souls; and, in the
future, the sower and the reaper will rejoice together.

And so the single thought or word — the manifestation of true life in the soul — which may go
forth from you or me, to-day or to-morrow; which
may be forgotten even by ourselves in a little while,
or of which, at the time, we may be ourselves unconscious — may enter the life and thought of another,
and, as it works through him, may go forth into his
future influence and thus perchance find a permanent
lodgment in some mind, after a season, which knows
nothing of our having ever lived, and whose sphere
of thought may be in a far distant part of the world.
But it was a word spoken or lived for the truth, and
the one who gave it forth, and the one who shall
receive it, find in it, alike, the same testimony : that
Jesus Christ is the way, and the truth, and the life.

As a force, also, in the souls of both, it is and will
be the same thing. We may be apart from each

other in our employments, in our mode of earthly living, in our associations, in our style of thinking, in our views of Christian doctrine even, in many respects. We may even misunderstand each other, and, from a half knowledge of the truth on either side, may contend, and pass condemnation, and sometimes lose out of our hearts, for a season, the love that believeth and hopeth all things. But the energy of that something which we gained through the Divine influence will enter into our souls underneath all peculiarities of our thinking or living — far below the sphere of our misapprehensions of one another and our earnest conflicts — and will move, in each one of us, along the lines of individual character toward the same ennobling of the soul, reaching out ever towards the perfection of true life. Peter and Paul contended; the Apostles were but partially enlightened in the early years; the truth in its fulness was beyond them. But Christ, the common Master, was the same. The work which His life-power did in them and for them was, also, the same. The influence which they passed over to the future was to the same great end. And the one thing, needful for all, was accomplished equally, and by the same power, for the humblest peasant in Galilee who entered in the earliest days into fellowship with Jesus, and for the most cultivated and honored saint who may have died, the last year, in a Christian country. The power was unto salvation in both cases alike.

I do not see how any thoughtful man, with his heart open to purest thought and influence, can read the simple story to which this suggestive verse belongs, and doubt afterward the final triumph of the kingdom; or how such a man can fail to believe that, in those early hours of communion with Jesus, the author of the record discovered that which transformed his living into an immortal beauty. And if the record of the reader of the story in the future is, like that of the writer of it, lost, as it were, in the words: "And one of the two that followed Jesus was Andrew, Simon Peter's brother," he will still find for himself in the hour of his first friendship with Christ the value of all life, and the glory of it also.

II

EACH MAN'S LIFE A PLAN OF GOD

Verily, verily, I say unto thee, when thou wast young, thou girdedst thyself and walkedst whither thou wouldest: but when thou shalt be old, thou shalt stretch forth thy hands, and another shall gird thee, and carry thee whither thou wouldest not. Now this he spake, signifying by what death he should glorify God. And when he had spoken this he saith unto him, Follow me. Peter, turning about, seeth the disciple whom Jesus loved following; which also leaned back on his breast at the supper and said, Lord, who is he that betrayeth thee? Peter therefore seeing him saith unto Jesus, Lord, and what shall this man do? Jesus saith unto him, If I will that he tarry till I come, what is that to thee? Follow thou me. This saying therefore went forth among the brethren, that that disciple should not die: yet . Jesus said not unto him, that he should not die; but, If I will that he tarry till I come, what is that to thee?

JOHN xxi. 18–23.

THESE verses of the closing chapter of John's Gospel present before us some of the last words of Jesus, which were addressed to two of His most prominent disciples. With reference to both of them the words apparently foretell something of their future career, and especially somewhat as to the manner of their dying. I propose to consider them as they may offer directly or indirectly certain thoughts and teachings.

19

The characters and work of the two men were very different. Peter, as he is presented before us in the New Testament, and according to the picture which we form of him, was full of energy, ardent, impulsive, ready for every new and worthy undertaking, practical, a leader for other men of action to follow. John, at least as we know him in his later years, was quiet, calm, thoughtful, dwelling more in the internal than the external, a lover of the truth and meditating upon it, rather than one who found his chief joy and satisfaction in the activities of the world. It is certainly suggestive to thought, if we notice what Jesus said to them, as connected with these differences, — especially if we bear also in mind what the future in each case proved to be, so far as the tradition of the Church has made it known to us.

In the first place, the manner of living and dying which is predicted for each of the two men is in accordance with the character of each. The man of fiery energy, and eager for action and conflict, had begun his career by the carrying out of his own impulses. He was the impersonation, as we may say, of youth, in his younger years, — pushing his way forward according to his personal will; a firm believer in himself and his own powers; arrested by no difficulties or opposition; determined to conquer and to succeed. The future for him, according to the ordinary laws of life, was to open toward greater conflicts and harder struggles. His very method of working would bring him into the midst of dangers and

20

enmities. He would rouse the evil passions of men, and excite them to throw every possible hindrance in his path, or even to contend against him with their deadliest weapons. In an age like that in which he lived and a work such as the one in which he was engaged, a man of his character would be peculiarly exposed to violent opposition. He would be as a single man contending against a thousand. The truth for which he strove was disbelieved. It was rejected by men of every class. It was hated by all who saw in it danger to their own systems of faith, or to their personal success or power. The career of such a man must be filled with fightings. In any period of the world's history, it must be liable to end in defeat for himself, if not for the cause which he advocates. But, in such an epoch as that in which Peter was living, defeat meant death, and that by violence. Jesus predicted only what might, not unnaturally, be expected, — that the time was coming when, having grown old in the conflict and in years, the ardent and active disciple, who had in his earlier life girded himself and moved whithersoever he would, would be overcome and led forth at the will of others, even to execution. He would glorify God by a martyr's death.

But equally in the case of the other disciple was the prophecy of Jesus in accordance with the natural movement and ending of a life like his. The calm spirit, which thinks and loves, — which tells its thoughts and shows its love, — awakens no violent opposition. It dwells apart from strifes, even if it dwells near the world's active life. It moves serenely forward, and the years go by. If the life chances to be lengthened out to extreme old age, and the mind is in its full power at the latest season, the passing on and the passing away may be but as the change of the daylight hour to the beautiful evening time.

The suggestion of the text, in this view of it, I think may be this: — that as, in the ordering of Providence, we are born with varying characters and gifts, and are assigned to different works for God in the world, so we may believe that there is a plan for every one, formed, and watched over, and carried to its completion by the Divine Friend who calls us into His service. How often we find, in our individual experience, that we never escape the besetment of peculiar difficulties or trials, which other men around us either do not have, or grow out of as the years move onward. We hope to escape them — we wonder that we do not, it may be — but we find them always with us. Is it not the Lord's appointment — not as an arbitrary or outward thing, but as a part and outgrowth of our peculiar nature? Is not the true way of looking at it this: that we — in our individuality of nature — were made for the accomplishment of a special Divine purpose; for the showing forth of a Divinely-formed character and life in one particular light; and that all allotments of experience are wisely fitted to realise the end? The work of Peter as a disciple of Jesus was intended to be different from that of John. He was to show the development of true life in a different way. The career followed the line of the native endowments. The trials and successes, the defeats and victories, as they were seen in the progress of his living and foreseen by the Master, were in accordance with what was foreshadowed in that manifestation of the Divine purpose which was seen in the making of the man.

We do not penetrate the heavenly wisdom, indeed, and we cannot say that this is a full account of what we call the Providential dealing with us. But may we not say that it is a partial one? And if it is so, surely it takes up all our living, and every part of our experience, into God's plan and purpose — and brings us the lesson of trust and confidence that the natural movement of our life, as we call it, is under a supernatural guidance, and that, in our allotment of every sort, and in the dying at the end, we are guarded and guided by a Father's love.

In the second place, we may notice what Jesus says to Peter in answer to his inquiry respecting the appointed destiny of his friend and associate. The manner of his own dying had been foretold to him; and now, as he sees this friend approaching, his mind naturally turns to the thought of *his* future. What of this man — what shall be his experience? The Lord answers, If I will that he tarry till I come, what is that to thee? There is in this answer nothing of definiteness, — at the most, only a suggestion that John's life would be longer and quieter than that of Peter himself. But the main word for the latter disciple is the pointed question, What is that to thee? with the bidding, Follow thou me.

23

What is the lesson given here? Evidently, as a
first part of it, that curious inquiry into what may
lie before our friends, or even ourselves, is not the
thing to occupy our minds. The appointed work
for us is, to follow the Lord, each one for himself.
Peter had, indeed, been told, as most men are not,
and even the other disciples were not, that a death
of violence was before him, and would come when
he should have passed within the limits of old age.
But the language used in giving him this assurance
was figurative in its character, and might naturally
suggest a career of trial and defeat, rather than its
ending only. Indeed the form of expression used
by the evangelist is such as to intimate that the
understanding of the words with reference alone to
Peter's death came to the minds of the disciples only
at a later period. As to the time and the particular
mode of dying, they were certainly indefinite. But
when the inquiry was turned to John's fate, the answer
was only with an *if*, and it revealed nothing beyond
the possibility of the Divine will. The *if* did not
gain its interpretation till the fact was realised —
nor, indeed, even then, for, if we may believe in any
measure the story which has come down to us,
many thought, after John had made the correction
which he gives, and after he had passed away, that
he was not dead, but was to live until the Lord's
second coming. Not questioning, but working, is
the Christian's duty; — this is the first part of the
lesson.

And a second part seems to be this: — that, in
the working, duty lies in the pathway of individual

capacities and powers. Peter was called to follow
the Lord in the line where, with his natural characteristics, he could best serve Him; the line which
would end, indeed, in martyrdom. But he was not
to be planning for martyrdom, or thinking of it.
The prophecy which foretold it was, at the most,
to be an inspiration to him in his career — for the
reason that the career was to end in a glorifying of
God after the manner in which Jesus Himself was
about to glorify Him. The following of the Master
was to be the object of his thought — a daily following, according as the way of service should become
manifest, and the way in which the Master would
have walked, had He been in his place, should be
made known. Think not of to-morrow, or the end,
is the teaching — think of to-day, and its work.
How simple the bidding was: Follow me. How
peaceful it was — The future belongs to God; it is
the object of His care and thought; it will be one
thing for one of his children, and another for another; and for both alike it will be but the following
out of that plan which He undertook to carry on
at the beginning. If each shall follow — to-day as
it comes, and to-morrow as it comes — the call of
the Lord, the ending will be provided for, and,
whatever it be, it will be a glorifying of God.

It is significant that this same bidding follows the
prophecy of Peter's death and the answer respecting
John's future. As if Jesus had said: When the
vision is given for a moment, and in a figure as it
were, of what is before thyself, let it only move thee
to a more earnest devotion to the duty which offers

itself at the same moment; — and when the sight of another's destiny is absolutely denied thee, still have the same earnestness. And so His last words to these two most intimate and beloved friends are the words which He uttered at the beginning of His public ministry: Live the right life to-day, and be not anxious for to-morrow.

What a wonderful peace there must have been in the inmost souls of these two disciples if they guided their lives by these words in the years which came afterward — the one moving on to his martyrdom, and the other to his quiet death and the falling asleep that seemed to those about him to be another thing than death, but both hearing the Lord's voice daily, saying, " Follow me," for the present; and, " What is it to thee?" of the future.

A third suggestion of the text is as to the true estimate which is to be placed upon different kinds of life. The praise of mankind is always prone to go towards those whose lives are passed, as we say, on the scene of action — the leaders of men in the struggle and warfare. But it is a striking fact, worthy of serious reflection, that it was not Peter, but John, to whom in the Divine plan the longest life was assigned. And this longest life was not mere living, but the accomplishing of a great work. Peter followed the Master, and did an honourable service, and glorified God, at its ending, by a death which corresponded with his life. But we may not forget that it was the meditative and thoughtful disciple — the one whom Jesus loved, and who

leaned on His breast at the supper — to whom the
last work of the Apostolic age was appointed. After
Peter and Paul had fulfilled their mission, he came
to finish what they had begun. And the message
which he sent down the ages is the most precious
inheritance of the Church. Peter is an interesting
character, but we know little of what He taught or
thought, in its distinctive peculiarities, and comparatively little of what he did. But the thoughts of
John give us the setting forth of the deepest
mysteries of the Christian truth, and let us into the
innermost secret of Christian living, and open before
us the heart of God, and read us lessons for which
the thoughts of the other greatest Apostles are only
preparatory. Our vision of the future places, as all
Christian thinkers hold, the Johannean age as the
final one in Christian development, and the disciple
of love as greater than those of faith and of hope.

The world is governed more by men of thought
than by men of action — when we take the great
progress of the ages into account — and it is so
peculiarly in Christian history, and above all in
Christian experience.

But the teaching of the text, in this line of thought,
is also that, according to the true Christian estimate, what seems the quiet, calm life, away from the
stir and strife of the world — withdrawn, perhaps by
necessity, from the great activities of mankind — is
a life as near, or even nearer it may be, to the heart
of Christ, than the one which is most conspicuous
in its Christian labours seen of men. It was the
meditative, loving disciple, whose work came after

the struggles and conflicts were over — the one whose life was longest, partly no doubt because he was outside of the tumult, and whose death was so like a sleep, — it was this disciple, whom the Lord loved, and to whom He committed the task of writing the story of His own Divine life among men, which should bear witness most fully of the Divinity and the humanity in their marvellous union. The believer who thinks and loves stands on an equality with the one who works and wars; Peter and John were together in that final interview recorded in this Gospel. He may even have a higher standing; as John was living after Peter and Paul had passed away.

We may also observe, in connection with the thought of the future of these two men as that future is hinted at in these verses, the importance to the Christian work in the world of the union of the two characters within the Church. The work of Christianity is to bring the world towards the perfectness of God. But the work is to be accomplished by human agencies and in human lives. The perfectness is therefore to be realised, not in any one individual, but rather in the combining together of the full developments in all. Each man is to manifest what the Divine power in Christianity can do for him. Were the more active virtues alone to be seen, the end would be but half secured. Were they not seen at all, the aggressive force upon the world would be mainly lost. But God has joined the man of energy and the man of quiet and thoughtful spirit, and given to each his own sphere of working for

Him ; — and if they follow along the line of His appointment, with no misunderstanding of each other, the result is reached — all combining for the common end, even as the writings of Peter and Paul, on the one hand, and John on the other, have made their way together into human souls everywhere, and transformed them from the earthly into the heavenly mode of living. And so the teaching of these words is that those who believe are to grow and work together, but not after precisely the same pattern, or in the same way.

I think we may fitly notice, once more, what I may call the incidental character of the words. The meeting of Jesus with the disciples on this occasion seems to have taken place almost by an accident. They had come together for an ordinary occupation, and apparently they were not thinking of Him, or of His possible presence with them. In the early morning, as they were in the disappointment of a failure of their work, He stands upon the shore, and gradually, and in a peculiar way, He makes Himself known. He teaches them of their office and their dependence upon Himself, and perhaps of the confidence which they may have in His aid whenever they put forth their efforts in His cause. This is what comes first and foremost. Then he seems to take this opportunity — because it chances to present itself — to call Peter's attention to his three denials, his threefold failure in love, and to ask him to look into his own character. But the object is not self-examination, but forgiveness; and so He

restores him fully to his office, committing to him
once more the care of the flock, and bidding him
feed and tend and shepherd all the sheep. Direct-
ing his thought in this way to his work and duty,
He easily and naturally speaks of what was awaiting
him in the future, and of the death which should
terminate his career. The allusion to the future and
the death of John was even more accidental, as it
were — occasioned simply by the fact of his happen-
ing to move along the path by which Jesus was
walking with Peter, and then by the chance question
suggested to Peter's mind by what he had heard
respecting himself. How prominent the thought of
the ending is as we look at the *close* of the chapter.
How secondary and subordinate, as we move towards
it from the *beginning*.

Is it not so with the ending of every life? In our
ordinary thinking of this ending, it seems like the
one great event, which gathers about itself all
solemnity, and seems to include within itself the sum
of all the past and all the future. But when we move
forward in our thought from the beginning and
through the life, it becomes an incidental thing — the
natural ending of the life whatever it may be ; — the
subordinate, not the principal event — subordinate
to duty and service and character, which are the
principal things ; — the passage-way from a living in
one sphere of activity to a living in another. And,
in this view of it, does not the question which was
addressed to Peter respecting his fellow-apostle come
with a Divine emphasis, and a Divine tenderness, to
each one of us with reference to himself: What is

it to thee? We enter upon the duties and struggles of our coming life — and the call from the Master is, Follow me. We know not the end, but it will be the end of service to Him here, and the opening of something higher and better than earth.

The writer of the Gospel closes the chapter in which this story of the two disciples is found with the words: And there are also many other things which Jesus did, the which if they should be written every one, I suppose that even the world itself would not contain the books that should be written. We may often wish that the words which He said might have been all preserved to us. But those which we have received are full of suggestion, and the thoughts of Jesus grow in their greatness and power within our hearts until they more than fill all the sphere of our living. The one word: Follow me, fills all the sphere of duty; and the one word: What is it to thee? commits the future to His keeping, and thus may give to us, each and every one, a perfect peace.

III

THOU SHALT KNOW HEREAFTER

Jesus answered and said unto him, What I do thou knowest not now; but thou shalt understand hereafter.

JOHN xiii. 7.

THESE words, as we read them in the connection of the verses, have reference to the particular act of Jesus which is here recorded. They assure the disciple to whom they are addressed that the meaning of what had just been done, though not recognised by him at the moment, would be unfolded at a later time, and they thus suggest to him that he should accept willingly and trustfully the service which was offered, and should be content to wait until the time of revelation should arrive. In themselves, however, and apart from the limitations of the passage and the occasion, they involve, as we may say, a great principle and law of our human life. They set forth before us the divine method of preparing the soul for its future, in one striking aspect of it. They read us a lesson which life itself enforces and emphasises as it passes on in its course. It is in this latter view of the words especially — and yet not without considering the former view also — that I would ask for thought and attention at this time. There are two leading suggestions which I would mention as connected with the words.

32

The first suggestion which the words bring to us, I think, is that of the Christian idea of life. It requires but a small and brief experience to lead any reflecting man to the knowledge and conviction that much of what befalls him is beyond his present understanding. The child's question, *Why*, is one which arises in this regard, as it does in others, very early in the child's thinking as to himself. It is a question which returns as the deeper thoughts of later years impress the soul, more and more, with the mystery of its movement along the line of its development, and the equal mystery of its surroundings. The wonder of our being — what life means; what it is and is to be; what are the design, if there be design, and the significance of the many strange things that enter into it, or perchance destroy it — becomes greater, the longer we study the matter. It reaches out into the wonderful to a longer distance, and to an obscurity which seems more impenetrable, as we come nearer to the end of what we think of as the allotted period of our living; so that the man of sixty or seventy questions, and meditates, and tries in vain to answer, many times and in many places, where, at twenty or thirty, he had not yet entered into the mystery, or had lost thought of it in the eagerness of his action or his hope. Thou knowest not now, is a truth which we all learn from the beginning onward, whenever we turn our thoughts inward upon ourselves, and then look out from within upon the future and its relations to the past and the present.

But the Christian idea goes beyond this. It does

not, indeed, reveal all things, and thus remove the
mysteries in the midst of which we are. This it
could not do, by reason of the limitations of our
vision. But it opens life to us as an education for
a future that follows it, and thus gives us the promise
which belongs to all education — that what is not
known to-day will be known hereafter — that the
steps forward which we take are steps bearing us
into the light, and so we have only to wait a little, or
to wait until the end, and the pathway which was
dark before us will be clear and plain behind us, —
and not simply plain *in itself*, but clear in its *leading
to the end*.

There is nothing more essentially connected with
education than this fact or law, of which we speak.
The beginner in any line of study or of art, as we
may all know by our own experience, must have
rules, and details, and imperfect and separate parts
placed before him. He must occupy himself with
these, and move in all his mental activity within
their sphere; and make them, as it were, to be of
his intellectual life and force, long before he can
appreciate their full bearing upon the result which
he proposes to accomplish. The work may oftentimes look forbidding and meaningless, as it is assigned to him to do, and he may be often ready to
turn aside from it as of no profit, or as never leading to anything of worth. He cannot see far enough
to understand what will come. But he must nevertheless hold firmly to the task, if he would not fail;
— and if he does so, after a season the separated
things will begin to come together, and take their

places in what is greater and wider than themselves.
They will combine with each other, and form a
whole which in its turn, and when it has served its
separate purpose, will unite with something else,
formed perhaps after the same manner, and thus
will grow ever towards the end of perfect knowledge. This is the way in which the mind always
works.

But it works *by the force of a promise*. The
teacher does not say to the child, simply or as the
chief thing: You do not know the purpose and
meaning of what I do, when I set your mind upon
the rudimentary details, and call you to the learning of rules or the drawing of lines. This also is
not what we say to ourselves when, in later years,
of our own choice we begin for ourselves some new
study, which may seem harder to us even than did
the studies of our childhood. The word which we
address to our own minds, and which the teacher
utters to his young pupil, is a word of assurance:
You will understand by and by. There is no impulse or moving power in the former word. It is,
moreover, understood well enough, and sadly enough,
by each one for himself, without the utterance of
it. But in *this word* there is hope and encouragement. In it is mental life. The faith in the future
becomes the evidence of the things not yet seen,
and the mind moves forward under the inspiration
of the thought that the faith will be, at some time,
changed into realisation.

The same thing is true with relation to character.
The child, in the formative period, is necessarily

35

subjected to laws of conduct and of thought, the significance of which he does not comprehend. They may seem to his mind to be merely arbitrary, and to bear upon nothing that is really good. And not only is it so with the child. We all, as we pass on to the years of self-control and self-government, find ourselves limited in a similar way. So long as we think only of the present and of the life which belongs wholly to it, the meaning of the rules which we obey is often lost to us — and men about us we see continually so losing it, that they ruin themselves by their neglect and want of understanding. But when character is looked at from the point of view where we regard it as developing for the future — its growth an educational process, and its value to be seen in the manhood which is secured — a new light shines for us. There may be still no adequate apprehension of what the disciplinary rules and duties mean; but the great fact that they point forward, and draw a life-power from what is beyond themselves, brings into them the element of prophecy and promise. We can now say to those to whom we would give our friendly help, or to our own souls in the working of their inner life: Give obedience at the beginning, though you do not yet understand. The rules will turn into spontaneous action, after a season, and will find the explanation which you ask for now, but are unable to discover, in the living forces of a strong and noble character. " Hereafter " is the great word of the mental and spiritual life. It is the characteristic word, as we may say, of such life, when viewed as having in

itself the element of growth, and as being, in its
early stages, a preparation for what is later. The
growing mind and soul cannot, from the nature of
the case, apprehend to-day, in its fulness, what may
be apprehended in some to-morrow, when there is a
larger development. But if there is an education in
each to-day for each to-morrow, and always for the
distant to-morrow, then the unknown of the present
seems to borrow from the knowledge of the future
an influence and vital power, which bear the man
forward intelligently and with confidence.

The Christian doctrine lays hold, as it were, upon
this thought, and makes life an educational period
preparatory to something greater than itself, yet like
itself. It conceives of the whole of the earthly life
as having a relation to the eternal future, similar to
that which the earlier part of the earthly life bears
to the later part. Life, according to its idea of it, is
one thing — one great and long development — one
grand movement from the beginning — never ceasing, ever growing in its power and in its progress.
To-day is for to-morrow; to-morrow for the next
to-morrow; the next for still another; and all for a
time which is beyond the boundaries of our earthly
planning or thinking — the time of perfected character in heaven.

In a peculiar sense and measure, therefore, does
it emphasise the "hereafter" of the text, and take
into itself, as what must characterise its whole conception of our human living, this fact: — that the
future is to understand the present, while the present does not, and often cannot, understand itself.

If we are born for an eternal existence — if the few years which we pass here are but the beginning of an endless future, and as if the early childhood of an ever-enduring manhood — surely we cannot expect to discover, in the days as they pass, the meaning of what meets us and bears upon our souls in these days. But *as surely* may we expect with confidence to find it afterwards. Life is education, all of it. Its significance is in the results of its growth. Its reality is its future. Its time of realization is when it can give, by reason of its progress, a look backward. And the more distant that time is, according to the true view of life, the more completely must this law of education manifest itself as the controlling, all-pervading law.

It is of the necessity of the Christian idea of life, that it bears this thought, of which we are speaking, with itself. But there is more in the Christian doctrine than this which has been mentioned. Life according to its view is not only the educational time, with all which this involves as bearing upon our present thought. There is something additional to this. The education is under the guidance of a Divine teacher, whose plan takes into itself all things from the beginning onward to the remotest future — a teacher also who is full of wisdom, and full of love. The mind which is moving forward through the years with limited powers is, therefore, under the direction and leadership of a mind which is unlimited. The limited mind may not know indeed, in the midst of the present experience, what the

teacher means or does, but there is no darkness or
misapprehension in the unlimited mind. Jesus said
to Peter: What I do *thou* knowest not now. He
does not say: *I* know not now. On the contrary,
His words carry in them the suggestion and assurance that He had this knowledge, and that He saw
the end from the beginning. If so, what must the
declaration have involved to the disciple's mind as,
after the surprise and bewilderment of that sorrowful evening had passed, he thought of it in the light
of all that he had learned of Jesus. He must have
seen in it the promise of an all-seeing Friend, who
was watching over and carrying forward the plan of
his personal life.

This word was spoken, we must remember, at the
end, not at the beginning, of the three years of their
life together. It was spoken at a time when the
wonder of the great Teacher's wisdom, and of His
insight into the soul and its life, and of His clear
vision of the future, and of the working of the present for it and towards it, and of His love for His
friends, had long been manifesting itself, and with
ever-increasing impressiveness. It was spoken thus
when the full light of Jesus' life was breaking in
upon the mind of the disciple. It must have meant,
therefore, to Peter's thought, that the progress and
growth of his own life were, and were to be, a true
education for the great future — with all the natural
movements, and all the privileges, and all the
promise, which such education, when under the
wisest and most loving teacher, can know as belonging to itself.

And what is this privilege and this promise in its highest form, but the certainty, that, as the man goes forward out of the present, where he knows not the meaning and deepest reality of that which he experiences, he will pass into a future of understanding — a future, not immediate perchance, but sure and blessed in its coming. The want of knowledge in the present, therefore, has in it no intimation of continued want. It cannot have such an intimation, when the word of Jesus is spoken. The darkness is not the deep darkness of the night season, in which there is no prophecy or hope. It is that which precedes the dawn of the morning, and into which the illumination of the approaching day seems to penetrate as each moment, in its passing, brings on the promised time.

The Christian doctrine is blessing everywhere. The gospel, in every aspect of it, is indeed good tidings. It lays hold upon life, in all its parts and possibilities, and shows it to be full of the goodness and the gifts of God. It glorifies life everywhere, by making manifest its relation to the future, and revealing the truth that, once begun, it never ends, but grows under the loving Teacher's and Father's care continually, ever attaining new and larger knowledge, greater and more ennobling virtue. And so *here*, it enters with its glorifying power into the limitations of our seeing and our knowing; and by telling us that our life is education, and telling us also who is the teacher, it seems almost to remove the limitations themselves by its assurance and the prospect which it opens. The childhood which is growing up under the unerring care and guidance of the loving Divine Teacher may be fettered in its understanding and apprehension, because it is still childhood. But the light is before it, and it may move onward hopefully, for the preparation to which it is called is a preparation for manhood — a manhood in which the past and the present will alike be full of brightness, and reality, and deepest and divinest meaning. Not now indeed, but hereafter. Yet the hereafter abides, while the now passes away — and the blessing is ever with that which abides.

We may now turn to the second and remaining suggestion which the words bring to us at this time — that of the wonderful and beautiful way in which, as these words show us, our lives are made to move forward in this education, and by the Divine Teacher. The plan develops itself in great wisdom, as we ourselves are brought to understand it.

Sometimes, as in the case of Peter when the words were first spoken, the unfolding of the meaning is given, partially or wholly, in the immediate future. Many have thought that it was given wholly to this disciple in the words which were added a few moments later. The washing of the disciples' feet was designed to teach the lesson of humility and service. If this was the fact in this particular case, it illustrates much that comes within the experience of every believer. How many times the thoughtful man finds himself suddenly arrested in his career for a moment, as Peter was, by what seems a strange thing, perhaps a small one, affecting himself. He knows not what it means. But it sets him upon thinking. The very strangeness of it makes him thoughtful of its bearing upon his character and inward life; and even as he medi-tates upon what it may possibly have to teach him, the light shines clearly, and the lesson is read in the light. He is ever afterwards, if he faithfully learns the lesson, more of a true man in one part of his living — it may be, a limited and narrow one, but yet one part — than he was before. Peter knew more of what this lesson of humility and service would teach, at the end of that memorable evening, than he did at the beginning of it; and we may well believe that the knowledge never failed him. Thus it is with all true men. There are persons in every Christian company — younger and older alike — who have realised such sudden for-ward-movements in their own history, when some unexpected thought or event has affected the life, because it brought with itself a teaching imperfectly understood, or perhaps wholly unknown before. Character starts into new and higher development from such starting-points, and the man gains strength for the future from the revelation that quickly follows a thing which, in itself, was at the most the wonder of a moment.

But the meaning of Jesus' words, as addressed to Peter, according to the view of many others — and not improbably their view is correct — was not exhausted in the simple application which He then gave them. There may have been a deeper and more far-reaching significance, which was to be

unfolded to the disciple by the events which followed that evening, and by the later experiences
of the subsequent years. And if this be so, how
truly, again, it answers to Christian history everywhere. The strange, surprising thing, which happened at a certain moment, and which seemed to
find some explanation of its meaning soon afterward, proves to have a deeper significance than
was believed. Time and experience show that it
has a wider teaching, and that it enters, by its
lessons, into the individual character at new points.
The voice which it utters speaks after it was supposed to have given its full message, and it is
heard in some other region of the soul's living.
The first thought dies away apparently, it may be,
when it has imparted its quickening influence to
the mind. But it becomes, in fact, the origin of
new suggestions, and new quickening power, until
the whole character of the man may be set forward.

A striking peculiarity of the teaching of Jesus,
which cannot fail to be noticed by every careful
student of the Gospels, is the suggestion of such
seed-thoughts, as we may call them. He said what
was above the present understanding of those who
heard Him, or what had wide-reaching application
beyond the teaching or the circumstances of the
hour. Nothing is more characteristic of Him than
this, as He appears before us in His conversations
with thinking men, or with His twelve disciples,
which are recorded in the Fourth Gospel. He
taught and spoke thus, because His teaching was
life-teaching, not that of the philosophers and the

doctors. Life-teaching, such as His, is always suggestive. It is always intended to plant itself in the
soul as a power, and to reveal its vivifying force
whenever and wherever it may. Hence it is ever
creative, and always a blessing. Hence also, it
always carries within itself the promise of the hereafter — a hereafter which may begin with a first
explanation in a moment or an hour, but which
may become richer in its gifts of understanding
for years, or even beyond the counting of years.

What an emphasis must have been given to the
teaching of service and humility in the mind of
Peter as he carried the remembrance of this act of
the Divine Friend through his after life. How
much, and how many things, it must have opened
to him, as he told the story of the Master to the
churches which he established, and as he found
the greatness and honour of his apostolic office to
be in the sphere of humble service to the brotherhood. Thus it was with the other disciples. John's
character, which was so rich and beautiful that it
has challenged the world's admiration, was, as we
may not doubt, the growth out of such seed-
thoughts. The richness of his inner life was the result of what Jesus had done and said, as this worked
its way into the recesses of the soul with a constantly new manifestation of that which was hidden
within itself at the first. And this is the beautiful
thing in the growth of all purest life. We are
placed by the Divine teacher in a school of thought
and character, as it were. We are assured that our
life is to be an education, pointing by the necessity

which pertains to it as such, to the future, and then we are left to the influence of the events, and the teachings, and the thoughts, which may be sent to us by the Master's will. Each one of these may become a seed for growth. Each one of them may be taken by us into our inmost souls, and may abide there as a force for the developing and perfecting of character. They may be forgotten for a while, or may seem to have finished their work for us. But they remain with perpetual life; and, like the half-forgotten knowledge or study of the past, they waken again for new influence and new uses when, in some unexpected hour, the soul's experience or need moves near them. And when they are thus awakened, the understanding of what they are, and what they have in themselves, becomes more complete; and the *hereafter* stands in yet more glorious contrast to the *now* of the beginning.

The thought of a verse like this is often understood as applying exclusively to the sorrowful things of life. But that to which Jesus here applied the words was no sorrowful thing. It was loving service. It was humility, one of the sweetest of all the virtues. Jesus was teaching lessons of character. He was, in all His words, giving the Divine idea of life. He was telling how the soul grows through the promise of the future — the assurance of knowing hereafter what it does not now know — and not only this, but of knowing the meaning of what now comes within its vision, or its experience, with *a depth of knowledge* which passes far beyond our present understanding. This is the way in which we are educated, according to the Christian method, and the Christian conception of life as an education. It is a wonderful way of growing indeed, and a beautiful one. Nothing can be thought of that is better or happier — a way in which all our experiences, and all that is done with us, or for us, by the Divine Teacher and Father may become more and more suggestive of the thought and feeling which strengthen character, and more and more full of meaning and of light, as the years move forward in their course. All things must work together for good for those who are in such an education for a perfected life in the future.

But one of the chief wonders of this wonderful process is seen in connection with the sorrowful things. In these things, some of the greatest forces for the building of lofty character are found. They tell the soul more of its deepest emotion, and its richest life, than the joyful things do; for truth, as it bears on the soul's growth, lies very near to tender feeling, and to that sense of dependence which comes with loss or trial. But the sorrowful things, like the joyful ones, point to the revelation of the hereafter, and when they are taken into the soul's thinking and its learning, they work towards the light. Nothing is more true in Christian experience than this. The man who, as the years have passed, finds himself already having attained to some large measure of true manhood, will always bear witness, that in these things was the largest influence which worked to the realisation of the

46

end; and the testimony will also be, that, in this way and for this reason, the sorrowful things became joyful ones in their result, and for the hereafter.

Thus as we leave our meditation at this time on these words of Jesus let us carry in our remembrance what they reveal of the Christian idea of life and of the promise of the ever-opening future, and let us place ourselves under the guiding wisdom of the loving Teacher, who always repeats to each one of us, in our limitations and our imperfect present knowledge: " What I do thou knowest not now, indeed, but thou shalt understand hereafter."

WHAT GOOD THING SHALL I DO

And behold one came to him and said, Master, what good thing shall I do, that I may have eternal life? And he said unto him, Why askest thou me concerning that which is good? One there is who is good: but if thou wouldest enter into life, keep the commandments. He saith unto him, Which? And Jesus said, Thou shalt not kill, Thou shalt not commit adultery, Thou shalt not steal, Thou shalt not bear false witness, Honour thy father and thy mother: and, Thou shalt love thy neighbour as thyself. The young man saith unto him, All these things have I observed: what lack I yet? Jesus said unto him, If thou wouldest be perfect, go, sell that thou hast, and give to the poor, and thou shalt have treasure in heaven: and come, follow me. But when the young man heard that saying, he went away sorrowful; for he was one that had great possessions.

MATTHEW xix. 16–22.

THE person who is represented in this brief story as coming to Jesus is brought before us in a very interesting light. He is a young man of high position, — Luke speaks of him as a ruler, — and of lovable character. He is one who has evidently studied the questions which most deeply concern us as men; the questions relating to the true life of the soul. He believes in the good, and naturally turns to one in whom he has seen the evidence of genuine goodness, or of whom he has heard as

teaching the way to attain it. He is honestly trying, and has been trying in the past, to lay hold
upon the blessing according to the rules which
have been set before him. He has meant to do
right, as he thinks, and thus to be right. He has,
in one sense at least, observed and kept the commands of the Divine law, as revealed to his mind.
But with all his doing and effort, he has not found
inward peace. The assurance of the life eternal,
which he seeks, has eluded his seeking. The
question of all significance is not yet answered.

Jesus often, in His ministry, met with doubters
and enemies. He was compelled to set His truth
before those whom He knew were unwilling to
receive Him, and to subdue within them a strong
opposition, before He could secure them for Himself. But here was no sceptic, and no open adver-
sary. Here was a man who was so hopeful of
finding in Him something to help and satisfy his
soul that, as one of the evangelists tells us, he ran
towards Him with all eagerness as He was going
forth on His journey. He would lay before the
new Teacher the want and difficulty which he felt,
and would trust that, peradventure, a light would
come from the words that should be uttered, which
would guide him safely to the desired end. Such,
I think, may be regarded as his real position. He
was, as one has said, an honest, though erroneous,
seeker after truth and life.

His education, however, had been under the
Pharisaic influences of the time, and while he
seems to have realised that there was something

beyond the mere perfunctory righteousness which many of these teachers taught, he still centred his thoughts, as they did, upon *doing*, rather than *being*. The gift of eternal life, to his mind, was to be the reward for the doing of some good thing; and as he did not seem to have attained it as yet, or the sure hope of it, as the result of what he had already done, he would learn, if possible, what the thing, till now unknown, was, which, being done, should carry within itself the rich promise of the future. "What good thing shall I do?" was his question. The good things to which I have devoted myself in the past have not proved sufficient. What is it that remains? Tell me where I shall find it, and the doing on my part shall be ready, in order that the happiness may follow.

The sincerity of the young man's spirit, and the rectitude and innocence, as men call it, of his life, were such that Jesus loved him, as the truest souls love all that is beautiful in character, even though the divinest beauty is not in it. But while He was thus moved towards affection for him, He saw that the essence of true living was not to be found in him, because he rested in *the doing*, and his thoughts did not go out beyond it, or into the deeper life within.

There are lovable and yet restless souls everywhere, I am sure, whose position in this regard is like that of the young ruler. They have seen the right, and in a sense desired it. They have set before themselves the eternal life as the great thing to be secured at the end, and have always felt that,

without the attainment of this reward, the life here
will prove to be a hopeless failure. They have, as
they thought, sincerely endeavoured to do the duties
of life, and thus to make the end their own. But
they have limited their thought and energy to the
sphere of action only, and have lost sight of the
sources from which action derives all good that
there is, or can be in it. And when they have discovered that peace has not come to their souls with
the doing of this good thing or the other, which has
just entered with its influence into their lives, they
are restless to find some new good thing, different
perchance from what they have known before, that
by the doing of this also they may gain the prize.
Lovable souls they often are in the earlier years, but
they are moving away from the true line of living;
and by and by, as if by a law of the soul's nature,
they lose out of themselves the lovable element more
and more, and become, at the best, mere men of
good works without any inspiring life-force — that
is, of works which are dead and valueless to the view
of every man who knows what the deepest life is.

We may next observe how Jesus answered the
young man's question. It is noticeable, in the first
place, that He met him on the ground of his inquiry.
He did not turn his thought to faith and repentance
directly, but, as the question had been with reference
to something to be done, He reminds him of the
sphere within which it is to be found. The keeping
of the divine commandments is the means by which
eternal life is to be gained. To do God's will, as it

is made known, is to secure the reward. And when the questioner, who is filled with the idea of some special and remarkable good thing as essential to the end, asks in reply, Which command, or as the expression more properly means, What sort of command — Of what singular and peculiar character is this command of which you speak, He simply points him to the well-known requirements of the law: Do not kill; Do not bear false witness; Honour thy father and mother. The way to life is not a far-off path. It lies before you, along the line of your daily living. Do the duty, refrain from the evil, which you meet from day to day. The answer was so simple that the man could scarcely understand it. I have been fulfilling all these things from my early youth until now, he says, but no peace has come. Tell me of something more and further — some great thing which is, at the same time, *the good thing*. But no — Jesus has only the simple words: Do not kill, Do not bear false witness.

The purpose of Jesus was to teach him the truth from his own starting-point. So long as you think of mere doing, there is no one great thing to be discovered. The sum of duty is the law, with its words which you think you have always obeyed. If you have not realised in your soul the blessing which you seek, you must ask some other question than this which you are thinking of. Life goes with the doing of the requirements indeed, but not with the doing as an outward act. The law is fulfilled in the spirit of it, and there is no keeping of its commands until this spirit rules and guides the soul.

The Christian teaching is like the teaching of the Master. It approaches all who would seek life in the mere fulfilment of prescribed duties as Jesus approached this ruler. They are ever asking for some new thing to be done, as they come to know that what has been done has failed. They persuade themselves that they are ready to do anything, however great it may be, and however much of effort and self-sacrifice it may require, if they can only have *the one thing* made known to them which will surely bring the result. The unsatisfied want of their hearts is ever asking where it is. But the Christian teaching constantly reminds them, that the old and familiar commandments are those whose fulfilment is required — that eternal life lies near to them ; and, in this way, it strives to lead their minds to some truer conception of what obedience unto life is — not mere doing the good thing, or turning away from the bad thing, but doing, or turning away, with the obedient and loving spirit. The same outward act may have two different characters, as determined by the presence or absence of this inward spirit; and, when determined in character by its presence, it takes hold upon the blessing, no matter whether in itself it be small or great.

We may well notice, also, the manner in which the test of his own character was placed before the questioner. Jesus did not set up some abstract rule or method of deciding what right character or good action is. He did not proclaim the truth in the case as a moral teacher or philosopher might do. But with that wonderful knowledge of the soul which He manifested everywhere, He adapted His words to the individual man before Him. He penetrated, as with divine wisdom, the secret recesses of this man's character, and taught *him personally* what he needed to be taught. Moreover, in doing this, He revealed him to himself. It was for this end, no doubt, that He dealt with him as He did. The individual soul was what Jesus was ever seeking; and whether the soul should be gained, as the result of the seeking, or should be lost, He desired ever to make it know itself and know its real attitude towards the truth. The young man was not told that, so far from keeping the commandments, all of them, as he supposed, he had in reality transgressed some of them, or failed in the right doing of the special things which they required. He was not reminded *in words* that he was self-righteous, or even that his mind was dwelling in the sphere of mere external acts. So far from this, which might have turned him away from Jesus, with a justification of himself, or into a determined opposition, and have accomplished nothing for the opening of his true character to his own consciousness, Jesus called his thought to a single action, which was connected with the peculiar condition of his own personal life. He was very rich and had great possessions, the evangelists tell us. Jesus bids him sell what he has, and give to the poor. If you desire to know the good thing to be done, or the thing which, in your individual case, will be the fulfilling of the commandments, Jesus says to him as it were, do this which the animating spirit of the law

in all its requirements calls upon you personally to
do, and then you may come and follow me to the
securing of eternal life. How central, as related
to character, do these words become to the one to
whom they are spoken. How clearly, in and of
themselves, and with the addition of no further
word, do they reveal to him the depths of his
inner self.

And so it is always with the Christian teaching.
It deals with the individual soul, and adapts its demands and lessons to each one for himself. There
is no call sent forth to every man to sell his property and give to the poor about him. The over-
powering love of riches may not be in the heart
of every person who has great possessions, or even
if it is present, it may not be the thing which determines the character and constitutes the turning
point of life or death. It was so in this young man's
case, and doubtless is in many similar cases. But
there may be, in many others, no such love of
wealth, and the turning point of character may be
elsewhere. Let it be where it will, however, there
is, at that point, some act or decision which is, in the
sense in which Jesus uses the words, the doing of
the commandments. And this, not because of the
value or life-giving power of the act in itself, but
because in the doing of the act at the demand of
righteousness and of God the man has born within
him the spirit which fills the law and gives it its
living force.

There come to each one of us some such critical
moments of decision and action, at which character

55

turns in one direction or another — and the turning, at such a moment, may involve all the future. These moments become tests for the soul. The thing involved in the divine demand may be not as great as that which is here mentioned by the evangelist — it may be of a very different character. But it will be a thing in which self is sacrificed, and the man is brought under the rule of love. If the sacrifice is refused, the nobleness of the soul gives way. The evil power gains new strength and, it may be, becomes ever afterward resistless. If the sacrifice, on the other hand, is willingly made, the soul finds the thing which has hitherto been lacking — the good thing which secures for it eternal life. So soon as this demand has been met, the way to go forward into the true and eternal life is opened; and the man has only to follow after the Master, as the impulse of his soul will move him to do, and to find the life where He found it.

The young man went away sorrowful. The test made him known to himself. He saw, in a moment, that he had not fulfilled the commandments, and that the life-principle was not within him. He saw also that, for the unwilling soul, the giving entrance to the life-principle was a far harder and more trying thing than the doing of the most difficult acts, and that, in asking for some great thing to be done, he had failed to comprehend the greater things of character and loving obedience to duty. He was brought into the life-struggle of the soul by the words of Jesus, and the victory, as he knew, was lost. He was grieved, but he turned away.

What a different thing life would have been for him in the future, if he had turned its course in the opposite direction! The words of the story are very suggestive in this regard. Jesus assures him that, if he will yield to the demand which carries for his soul the life-forces within itself, he will have *at once the great possession*, in place of *the great possessions*. The eternal life is not simply an inheritance to be bestowed and waited for. It is something to be gained in the very fulfilment of the required duty. And this, because it is life. The act is nothing in itself, as we may say, — hard as it is, it is a mere doing of one thing rather than another. But in it the mind and purpose turn from selfishness to love, and the man is changed. Yesterday the man was moving downward, in the controlling impulses of the soul, but now he begins to move upward. The life-principle was at the point of the action, and the movement follows where the principle impels, just as the stream flows westward, or eastward, as the fountain turns on the mountain summit. Life moves, indeed, and grows afterward, and takes into itself all that may naturally belong to it, and reaps continually its own reward; and thus there is progress, and gradual development, and slow advance, as it may seem to be, towards a distant future. But, nevertheless, it has at the beginning what it has at the end, *its own vital power*, which is the reward.

And so Jesus says to the questioner, in the very words of His sentence: not, Give to the poor and then follow me; and thou shalt find at the end a treasure in heaven; but, Give to the poor and thou

shalt have the treasure in heaven ; and Come, follow
me. The assurance of the heavenly treasure — that
is, the true and eternal life of the soul, with all the
blessings which it does, and may, involve — is thine
already, when this act of giving, which is the turning act of the life, is done. What thou mayest do,
and wilt do joyfully, after the moment of turning, is
to follow me.

The whole thought and idea of the young man,
as he approached Jesus with his earnest inquiry and
with his hope of gaining light from Him, were mistaken from the very foundation. His mind had
been moving, as the minds of many like him even
in this age, to whom we have alluded, are now moving, in the sphere of the legal system and of reward
for works. But discipleship to Christ is not a long
labour, or a long pathway, at the end of which we
secure a reward in *payment* for what we have done.
It is a life which has its inheritance *as its birthright*
at the outset, and moves forward in the conscious
possession of it. In this sense it follows, rather than
precedes, the attainment of the end. It is a movement along the line of true living, which begins
from the self-propelling impulses of a new life. It
is a learning from Christ; a service and imitation of
Him ; a following after Him as the great Master
and Teacher, because in Him is manifestly set forth,
in its perfectness and glory, this life into which the
soul has newly entered. And thus the turning to
the new life — whatever may be the special act of the
man in the doing of which it takes place — is always
a joyful turning. It takes into itself the joy which

Jesus meant to have the young ruler take, when He said to him: Sell that thou hast and give to the poor. The young ruler's countenance fell as he heard the saying, and he moved on into the future sorrowful, because he had turned backward along the old course of his living. But there was nothing like this where Jesus pointed him. There was the beginning of a new life-force there, just within his grasp — just ready to be the inspiration of all his future existence — just waiting to give him the blessing to which no sorrow is added. There was a new life there, which should be, like all true and beautiful life, full of joy because full of its own activity; growing stronger and richer because of the continual forth-putting of its own powers; realising ever more and more fully the greatness of the inheritance, the possession of which it knew to be an essential part of itself at the moment when it began to know its own being. The treasure becomes yours when you turn toward God, instead of turning away from Him — such is the *meaning* of the words addressed to the young ruler, as they go forth beyond him to all who ask the question which he asked — the treasure becomes yours so soon as you turn toward God, instead of turning away from Him. Come, is the *invitation*, learn what the treasure is in its joy and blessing, by following after Christ.

And now, as we have followed out the line of thought thus far, we find a suggestion as to the significance of the words which seem strange to us at first, and with which Jesus opens His part of the

conversation: — Why askest thou me concerning
that which is good? One there is who is good.
The Christian message does not come to teach us
what is good, as if this had never been revealed to
men before. The good lies in the fulfilling of what
God commands — that is, the expression of His
will, which is the outcome of the perfect life within
Himself. Do the will of God, and become like
Him. This is the fundamental truth of all soul-life.
But this is a revelation of God in the consciences of
men, and in the law which was given long ages before the coming of the Gospel. Jesus was not a
new teacher, in the sense in which his questioner
seemed to look upon Him as such — a teacher who
could add to the old commandments and services
some one great thing, in the doing of which the
secret of life and peace was to be discovered. His
purpose and work were to a different end from this.
He came only to point the way, and to open the
way to God — to bring the soul back to that start-
ing-place of life, as it were, where with a newly
awakened and efficient life-force it could successfully
begin the work of true, loving obedience. Therefore, His bidding to this young man was: Do the
commandments — the simple, plain, old commands
of the law: not to kill, or steal, or bear false witness
— but do them, not as you have been doing them,
but with a full sense of their meaning and with the
spirit of God's children. To give you this sense
and this spirit, which you have lost out of yourself,
as you will realise in your own mind in a little while,
when I call you to give up your possessions for the

help of the poor around you, — to make you this gift was the purpose of my coming to you as a teacher. To receive this gift should be the purpose of your coming to me. Do not call *me*, Good Master — none is good save one, that is, God. Do not ask *me* respecting the good. One there is, who is good — the Divine Father. Let *me* only reveal you to yourself, and open your mind and your way to *Him*. My doctrine is no new commandment; it is the old commandment which was from the beginning. My words are spirit, and they are life. Take them into yourself, and you are a new man. The secret of the life which you desire is in the life-force.

We come thus at this point to the central truth. The Christian doctrine is not a revealing of what the good is, as if this had never been made known before, but a revealing of the way to attain it. The good is righteousness. The good is conformity in the life to the will, and thus to the character, of the one Being who is good — that is, God. But how shall we gain it? This is the question which we need to have answered for us, and Christianity gives us its answer.

It is worthy of notice, as we take leave of the story and its thoughts, how completely this answer turns the man away from self and selfishness. Jesus bids the young ruler seek after the good, which brings life and is life, in God. He is to find what he asks for in a personal communion with the source and author of the wonderful gift. He is to attain to this communion by a fulfilment of what is required as the essential element of true action and life; — and this fulfilment is to be the result and outgrowth of that principle of love which is the opposite of all selfishness. He bids him, again, in his movement towards fulfilling the law, to do those things which the law requires in his relations to his fellow-men. Do no ill to those about you, but ever do them good. Have that loving spirit within you, the out-flowing of which is service and helpfulness, and thus abide in the sphere of that golden rule of life which *inspires you*, while it *commands you*, to do to others as you would have them do to you. In this way, take the demands of the Divine law, as it was given at the beginning, into the deepest and inmost part of your soul, and make it the spring and fountain of all good deeds. He bids him, once more, to follow after Himself. Come, be my disciple — not as asking me one question, or how to do one thing, and then going away to depend on yourself, and to deceive yourself with the thought that you are obedient to the law — but, as a true follower in the way of the soul's true life, imitating, trusting, believing in, and yielding the soul, with its active powers and its loving powers, to the Teacher who will lead you away from the evil that is in yourself towards and into that good which dwells, in its fulness, in the one God. And so the bidding and the lesson are from the beginning to the end the same. Let him deny himself and follow me. Let him gain his life by losing it, and let him receive the hundredfold reward in the eternal good — which is the perfected soul, perfect in love — through giving up all that centres the soul in its selfishness and itself.

How clearly the lesson gathered itself into one word and one act, when Jesus said, Go, sell that thou hast, and give to the poor, and thou shalt have treasure in heaven. The life in the lower sense would be lost in the moment of the doing of that act, and the life in the higher sense would be gained at the same moment, because the act was so central, as related to the life-forces, that it carried within itself the change for all the future. The same is true of us. There is somewhere, for each one of us, a movement towards God which takes hold of loving trustfulness in Him, and is the beginning of the eternal life. It is a movement which answers to the inviting and teaching word of Jesus, and is ever afterward a following after Him. The supreme moment of our life-time is the moment when this word is spoken. The question of the eternal good for us is the question of our yielding to the call and bidding of the Master, or our turning away. The young ruler heard the word, and sorrowfully went to his old life once more. But the true life-forces were not to be found in the old path; and his going away was a far more sorrowful thing than he thought.

V

THE HEAVENLY VISION

Wherefore, O King Agrippa, I was not disobedient unto the heavenly vision. — ACTS xxvi. 19.

THE conversion of the Apostle Paul from his Jewish belief to his Christian faith, from his bitter enmity against Jesus to an all-constraining love for Him, and from an old life of harassing inward struggle to a new life of inward peace, has always stood forth in the history of the Church so conspicuously as to arrest the attention of every serious mind. The suddenness and the completeness in the change of the man bear witness of a remarkable power putting forth its energy, the reality of which it is impossible to deny. One day a persecutor; the next day a preacher; and the great transformation taking place by reason of a wonderful light breaking forth at noon-day — there must have been something in the scene and event, the reader of the narrative is impelled to say, which had a marvellous, if not mysterious, force for character and life. There must have been behind what was made manifest to the bodily eye, or in the centre, as it were, of that which was revealed to the senses, a life-moving element for the soul. The man does not become a new man — the newness does not make itself known as absolute and immediate — unless new and mighty energies are in movement at the hour. The wonder of the result proves the wonder of the cause, and there is no room for doubting when the result appears. Life testifies unmistakably of what lies back of it, for life is itself the movement of living forces.

It cannot but be interesting, if we are interested in Christian history and experience, or even if we are interested, as every manly man must be, in the condition and possibilities of the soul within us, to look into what the person who had this great change in his own life said about it, and to interpret his words by what we know of him after the hour of the wonderful scene.

The words of the verse which is taken as the subject of our thought give us *the cause* of the change, and *the working force* in the life that followed it. We may look at the words from the two points of view.

The cause of the change is represented in the expression: the heavenly vision. What was it, that was seen? It was a person. The Apostle saw Jesus. The wonderful man concerning whom he had heard so much, but in whom he had had so little disposition to believe — whose career he thought to have been ignominiously and disastrously ended by His ignominious death, and whose influence he doubted not would cease, so soon as His few followers could be scattered or suppressed — appeared in a marvellous way. He manifested himself as still alive; as exalted to a higher position, and higher power; as standing in close relation to His disciples; as planning for and ordering His cause in the world; as uniting in Himself and in His thought the heavenly things and the earthly, now that He had passed from the latter to the former. He stood forth clearly as what He had claimed to be, and as what those who had trusted Him supposed that He was — the divine messenger and Messiah sent from God.

But there was something beyond this, and something which was even more and nearer to Paul's personal life. The wonderful man declared Himself to be affected by what he had individually been doing. The persecution of His followers had not found its end in them; it had reached Him. The attempt to destroy the new belief was, in reality, an attempt put forth against Him who had awakened it. The onward movement in the line which Paul had chosen, and along which he was pressing so determinately and earnestly, was a movement in opposition to Him whose voice called to another line of action and another manner of living. There was a revelation of one personality to another personality, involving all which the one could reveal to the other. I am Jesus — so the voice said; — What am I to you, and what are you to me? These were the questions and thoughts which the scene brought to the mind of the one who witnessed it. They were thoughts to be dwelt upon, and questions to be answered, in the meditations of the years that followed, as well as in the first thinking of the present hour.

This is the representation of the matter which the Apostle gives in both of his two descriptions of the vision recorded in the narrative of the historian, and in all the passages of his own writings, also, in which he makes allusion to it. The sight which he had was a sight of Jesus; and the moving force for life was the force which came from His personality. We miss the very essence and central significance of the whole matter when we view it in any other way. The Apostle was not, as related to the great and remarkable change which took place in his inmost life, a man of reflection, or a philosopher, who had long been searching after the true doctrine of righteousness, and had finally reasoned out for himself the doctrine of faith. Much less was he one who, having been dissatisfied with all experiments and experiences which he had known in the past, had suddenly, as it seemed to himself at the moment, though probably not so afterwards, come to the conviction that the way of faith was the only way to attain forgiveness and salvation. His mind, even in the after years, when he became a great teacher of the churches, — much as it had to do with doctrine, or dwelt upon it for the benefit of others — never had the real movement of its living powers in the sphere of doctrine. This movement was in the sphere of personal living. All new thoughts which came to him — all new revealings — were of life, and for life. The doctrine entered through the door of the life, and was a secondary thing, while the life was primary. It was but the setting forth in words of the way in which the living begins and goes for-

ward — useful for its purpose, but not the first and
all-important and all-embracing thing. Life was
this all-important thing. It was so as truly in the
earlier days as it was in the later days. The deeply-
implanted and fundamental characteristics of the
man were not altered as the strange light shone in
upon him. The same enthusiasm for living, as distinguished from everything else, was in him at the
first, and remained in him. The line of its outgoing
only was, in the later time, a new one. The purpose of the man at the first, as always, was a purpose of life, and to the movement of life, and of
its forces, all his thinking was wholly subordinate.
The fact that it was thus, made the suddenness and
the wonder of the change possible. There could be
no great visions and revelations for such a man,
except visions and revelations for personal life.

How was it, then, that Paul saw the truth, or the
way of life and peace for his soul? He saw, in the
sudden light of the moment, what the other disciples
had seen in the years preceding. He saw that in
Jesus the Divine Father was manifesting Himself in
relation to men as His children, and that thus, in and
through Jesus, he could come into personal relation
to God as his Father. The whole matter of life for
himself was thus changed at once for his thought.
He was not living, as he had supposed himself to be,
under a system of rules appointed for him by a
governing power, in which the starting-point of all
action was within himself, and through which nothing but law moved towards his soul. He was living

68

under a system, though he had not realised it at all, of personal love. The voice which called him was a Father's voice. Because it was so, it carried the offer of forgiveness in itself — a free forgiveness, full and without conditions — immediate, and not dependent on a previous testing of long-continued action. Because it was so, it bore witness of loving trust as the uniting and re-uniting power which should bind the soul to God — uniting, where no sin had entered to break the union; re-uniting, where there had been such an entrance. How strange that he had never, before this, seen the truth! How beautiful it seemed, now that he saw it!

The words were very few, and very personal words: I am Jesus, whom thou persecutest. I am the messenger of God bearing to you, and to all men, the message of the Divine love, and you are resisting the message and persecuting the messenger. I place myself now before you, and place you, also, before myself. Think what we are, in our relation to each other — how you ought to feel towards me, and how you are feeling. You are moving in the wrong direction — wrong in a sinful way. You are acting as an enemy to one whom you ought to love — to one who has said all things and done all things in love to you. The soul's life is not, and cannot be, found where you are moving. It is not in enmity, but in love. How can you find your way back to it? By the pathway, and the only pathway, in which souls move into union — the pathway of loving confidence, the pathway of faith. Turn back upon your course and into this way; and forgiveness and peace will meet you at once. They will meet you at once, for I am in the pathway, and the Father is in me.

Such were the thoughts that the voice brought to him. They were involved in the words which were spoken. They bore in themselves a revelation which included everything for the man's personal living. They constituted, as we may truly say, the vision, for in the sight of Jesus, as the vision made Him known, they were opened to the mind. It is no wonder that they came in a moment, or that they changed the whole of life for the man who received them into his soul. This is the manner in which great life-thoughts come and work — oftentimes, if not always. Every true man knows somewhat of such experiences in his own mental and moral development. That is a beautiful story — as real in the history of the soul as it is beautiful in the telling of it — that story of the Prodigal Son, which Luke has recorded for us among the sayings of Jesus. It gathers up and centres in itself the gospel-teaching of forgiveness and life. But of all the wonderful and real things suggested in it, there is nothing more impressive for our thought than the suddenness of the new revelation for *the soul's life,* which came to the returning son when he saw his father in the pathway. He had before this, in all the seriousness of his mind which followed what the writer of the Gospel calls his coming to himself, been thinking of action beginning on his own part, and of earning favour by good deeds in the future, and of full reconciliation and restoration to the old tenderness of love on the father's side, when he had proved, by days or years of better living, his right to be trusted. But as the father stood before him, suddenly and unexpectedly revealed, the vision opened to him the inner life of the man whom he saw, and at the same moment opened to him also a new understanding of the relation of his own inner life to the life which he saw. He apprehended, as through the breaking forth of a light from heaven, that the renewed union of the two souls was to be secured through loving faith, to which immediate forgiveness answered, and thus that the life-pathway was the plainest and easiest of all pathways — with forgiveness and trust meeting each other at the very beginning of the path.

Paul was not a man like the prodigal, indeed, — far from it, — but he had the same revelation of the true life-way, and it came with the same suddenness, and after a similar manner. The old thinking gave way before the new vision. The new vision was the vision of the personality of him who was revealed in the one case as truly as it was in the other, and it carried in itself, in both cases alike, all the forces of the changed life. These forces were loving trust on the one part, and loving favour on the other — a thing on each side which the man had not comprehended before, but which, when comprehended, could not but stir, for all the future, the deepest thoughts of the soul.

The reasoning, the arguments and proofs, the development of the true doctrine, the unfolding of the plan and system of the Divine working for the re-

newed life of men — all this belonged to a later
season. All this had relation to the mind's thinking
and to the presentation of the truth to others. It
needed the growth of thought out of the first seed-
thought. It could wait for a time till the coming of
its own appropriate hour. But the man, at this
critical moment, was in another sphere. He was in
the great personal crisis for himself. He needed
only — and imperatively — the seed-thought, which
should have its growth afterwards. This seed-
thought was connected with the relation of his own
personality to the Divine personality, and it required
for its coming to the man, and its implantation
within him, one thing alone — the meeting of the
two personalities. The vision realised this meeting.
It had in itself the *cause* of what followed in the after
time, but did not gather into itself *everything* that
followed, whether in thought or in act. The soul-
movement which it knew as a real experience set in
motion the mind-movement and the life-movement,
but these in their completeness became real experiences only when the after-time had come. The
cause was not the effect; but it produced the effect.
What pertained to the vision was not the *whole* of
the *changed life* of the future; but it was the *whole*
of the *change*, out of which the future naturally, and
as by a necessity, came into being. It was, as life-
changes are, the matter of a single momentous hour
which centres all in itself.

Such was the cause of the change. The working-
force, by which the cause of the change was con-

nected with the result, is also indicated in the words
of Paul. Let us look at this for a few moments.
" I was not disobedient to the heavenly vision."
I did not resist, but I yielded myself to the influences which came to me from it. How simple and
natural it was! The son met his father in the pathway, as he had not thought of meeting him. At
the moment of the meeting, he saw in the father
what he had not thought to see. The revelation
was as distinct, and as complete, as it was unexpected. It opened an entirely new view of life and
its forces. It revealed love, and forgiveness, and
far-reaching possibilities, and wonderful hopes.
But there was a further revelation for the son's
life which came forth from that of the father's
life. It was the revelation of a new impulse
within himself, which was to make the life's movement afterward an easy one, and which would
prove a uniting power linking the cause of the
changed life to all the results. The impulse was
that of obedience to what the vision carried in
itself. The vision for Paul bore witness that the
Divine Father's love was ready, with a boundless
readiness, to forgive and pass over the past at the
very moment of the first turn in the soul's attitude
and feeling. The impulse of his manly soul was
to meet the love on God's part with an answering
love on his own. The Friend who had stayed him
on his journey through the suddenness and brightness of the light from heaven, had said all things
in testimony of love and of the Father when He
said, I am Jesus whom thou art persecuting. The

73

response could be no other than it was: What
wilt thou have me to do? The reconciliation,
which terminated the old life for him and began
the new life, was a change from enmity to love on
the one part, *because* of the overflowing fulness
of love on the other — and the impulse of the new
life was inseparable from the life itself.

We look along the course of the life-time after
that hour, and we see the new force working everywhere, and at all times. No sooner had the vision
passed, in the wonderful effect which it produced
for the moment, than the carrying out of the obedience to it began. In the very city to which he
had directed his way that he might accomplish his
hostile purpose, destroying the faith in Jesus if
this should be possible, he begins to tell of Him
as the hope of the soul and the power of God.
The movement of his energy is, at once, in entire
contrast to what it had ever been before. He
cannot be earnest enough to satisfy his own desires
and to meet with fulness of result the obligation
which he feels. The years pass on, and it is ever
the same. The sentiment of his life is expressed in
the words which, at the middle point of his career,
he addressed to the Corinthian believers: "The
love of Christ constraineth us, because he died for
us all; and he died for us that we should no longer
live for ourselves, but for him." These words were,
in reality, the remembrance of the vision. They
contained in themselves the essence of its meaning, and, by their living presence and power within
his soul, caused it to abide with him always. So

he passed from city to city — so he preached to
Jews and Greeks — so he made his defence before
the high-priest and the emperor — so he endured
all sufferings and trials — so he fought the good
fight and kept the faith — so he finished his course,
as he had begun it, with the one principle always
triumphant in his soul, the principle of love for the
one who had loved him and manifested Himself to
him.

This is the way in which life moves, when it is
impelled by a great and grand impulse, taken into
himself by one man by reason of his meeting with
another. But the peculiar expression of the Apostle
is worthy of notice, and it has a revelation in itself.
"I was not disobedient." He does not say, I put
forth mighty effort; or I roused my energy anew
by daily and continual awakening; or I stirred
my enthusiasm by the thoughts of duty or of success; or, even, I was active in obeying what I
seemed to have heard. He says simply, I was not
disobedient. The vision was a beautiful one, a
wonderful one. It had in it all thoughts of God in
His relation to my soul. It revealed to me Jesus
and all that is in Him. It set before me Jesus and
myself in the meeting together of the two personalities. There was but one thing needful for me to
do — and there never has been but this one thing,
from that far distant hour of my seeing the vision
to this late hour of my telling of it — and that was
not to resist its teaching and its influence. If I did
not resist these, the power for the life came forth of
itself. If I let it come, in the early or the late

hour — in the one equally as in the other — it came directly, easily, sweetly, with heavenly naturalness, to my soul, and showed itself in every way to be fitted for my soul. So I have worked on, with never-failing earnestness and with boundless enthusiasm, simply keeping the door of my soul open to receive what the vision ever held within itself for me. This is the story of my life, and now, as the end seems to be drawing near, and I stand before the great earthly powers awaiting their decision as to my fate, I am calm and peaceful in my memory of the vision and my thought of what it has done for me. I am even doubtful as to what I may wish to be the result, for I find, with an ever deepening sense of the reality of the experience, that it is Christ for me to live, and I know, with an ever growing confidence, that it is Christ in me, and with me, if I die.

This, my friend, is Christian experience from the beginning to the end. I commend it to you, that you may make it your own. The vision of Jesus is before you, if you will only open your eyes to behold it. You may see it to-day, if you will retire into the depths of your own soul and let your true personality meet His. The vision will be a more beautiful one than you ever saw before. It will have the great revelation of life for you. It will have in itself the life-power and the life-impulse. And the impulse which moves all forces within you will come into your soul, at the first, — and ever, again and again, through all the years — if you will only not be disobedient to the vision, but will suffer it to be for you what it truly is. The marvel of the Divine impulse for noblest living is, that it enters the soul *of itself*, when the vision is seen and the man opens the door. It is the working-force of the changed and renewed life, whose source is the love made known in the vision. It starts all energies and activities; moves to duty and endurance; gives strength for labour and trial; stirs the manhood to enthusiasm and heroism; makes life to be full, and great, and victorious everywhere. But it comes itself to the man gently and easily, asking of him nothing but that the door may be opened to receive it. It is breathed into his open soul with the breathing of Divine love, even as Jesus breathed on the earliest disciples when He met them on that first Sunday evening, and said, Receive ye the Holy Spirit. The effort, the struggle, the victory, come with the years, and along the years. But they all grow out of the impulse. It takes care of them and secures them; and, as it does so, it makes life strong, and manly, and ready for the present and the future alike. Let it enter in its own sweet way, through your seeing the heavenly vision, and not being disobedient to it. The life-time that follows will be ever realising more fully for you, and within you, what the life has in its possession and its promise.

It is a very significant circumstance connected with these words of the Apostle, as here recorded, that they were addressed to a man who had no interest in the speaker except that of curiosity, and no openness of mind at all for the doctrine which he declared. The man said to him a few moments later, in a tone half of pity and half of contempt: It is with a very little of persuasive power that you are trying to make me a Christian. Your visions, as you call them, have no meaning for me. They have, as I believe, no reality for yourself. You are a dreamer — a dreamer even to madness. My old faith, or my no faith, is better than this; and I have known too much of life to trust to such dreamings.

Paul made the answer which came from the inmost soul and from the soul's deepest experience: I would to God that not only thou, but also all that hear me, might become such as I am. *What I am* is *the reality* of the vision. Life-power, which transforms, and builds up, and new-creates the soul, pertains to no dreaming. It is the most actual and vital of all things. It comes to the soul, when it comes from another as it came to me, not from the picture of the man, or the dreaming of the man, but from the man himself. Call to mind what I was in the early days, and what I am now — think of what I was just before the vision, and what I was just afterwards; — and you may know for yourself what the vision had in it — reality and vital force — the cause and moving power of all that followed.

And this is the Christian testimony, which every believer has for himself and for the doubting or hostile world. I saw the vision, and it made me what I am. The growing years, since I saw it, have witnessed the growing life. The forces of the growing life are still working, and they are making

78

the man. The man within me, that is made, is the reality of all realities. No dream has made it. Dreams fade away and die. No empty vision has made it. The empty vision passes into nothingness. It was the meeting of my personal soul with the personality of Jesus which accomplished the result, and is still accomplishing it. I am not yet what I might be or ought to be — the years have not wrought in me all that the vision would, if unhindered in its influence, have realised. But I am something, and more than I once was, in the life of the soul that is worthy of the vision; and from the depth of the realised experience within myself I say to each and every one, I would to God that you all might become, in this regard, what I am. The life which I now live, I live in faith, the faith which is in the Son of God, who loved me and gave Himself for me. It was a beautiful vision. It is a glorious reality. The love and the impulse came from the vision, and they make the reality. They will make it for you, as they have made it for me.

So the Christian stands in the world, ever bearing witness as the Apostle did. His witness has in it a Divinely-given power, and it testifies for the truth of revelation and of experience.

IN NOTHING BE ANXIOUS

*In nothing be anxious; but in everything by prayer and sup-
plication, with thanksgiving, let your requests be made
known unto God. And the peace of God, which passeth all
understanding, shall guard your hearts and your thoughts
in Christ Jesus.* — PHILIPPIANS IV. 6, 7.

THE Epistle from which these words are taken
was written near the end of Paul's life, within
the two years of his stay in Rome, the reference to
which is found at the close of the Book of Acts.
There are many evidences in the letter that he had
gathered into his heart the lessons of a life-time, and
was now in the calmer and quieter mood of advancing age. He says that he has learned in whatsoever
state he is, therewith to be content; that he knows
how to be abased, and how to abound; that he can
do all things through Him that strengtheneth him;
that he forgets the things which are behind, and
presses on beyond them towards the goal; that he
is willing to have the Gospel preached, whether it be
by those in sympathy with himself or those strongly
opposed to his views, if so be that Christ is pro-
claimed; that he is ready either to live or to die, as
may be best for the cause. These things are, all of

them, utterances which come more naturally from one who has been long engaged in the struggle of life, and to whom the ambitions, the hopes, and the victories of the earthly warfare are becoming less powerful in the soul than they once were. Paul did not lose his energy, or his consecration to the work of Christ, as the years carried him forward beyond the age of sixty. But life became a different thing from what it had been at his entrance upon his labours; and he looked upon it from a different standing-place.

It is certainly fitting, and may well be a matter of interest, to contemplate him as he comes to this quiet Christian feeling at the later period — developed, as it was, so beautifully, and so much more fully than it could have been before. The life under the educating influence of religion does not remain always at one stage, or in one condition, but it grows into greater richness and deeper power as it moves on from period to period, until it passes into the perfectness of heaven. But, as it is ever growing, it gains the truest views in the later season — unless it suffers other and evil influences to becloud the clear mental vision.

The verses which have been chosen as the subject of our thought contain a most appropriate suggestion for a rule of living, and one which gains an especial force because it comes to us from the earnest and ardent Apostle in the calmer and later period of his life. I know of nothing in all literature which gives such a picture of what our feeling and action ought to be, or is a more beautiful motto for every man.

In nothing be anxious. This is the Apostle's reflection of the words of Christ in the Sermon on the Mount, Be not anxious for the morrow. But it bears the testimony of Paul's own life to these words. The words suggest what he deemed life to be, in the right view of it; and I am sure that we must hold that he saw the truth. The view of life here on earth which he had was, that it was a service like that of a commissioned agent, or a soldier. The plan of all working was not in the soldier's mind. It belonged to his leader. Labour and duty, therefore, were the things for him; results pertained to the sphere of another. Now anxiety begins when the soldier or servant allows his thought to go beyond his appointed work, and when he demands for his happiness success in his own part of the field, and not merely success in the whole undertaking at the end of all the conflict.

We see how Paul looked upon the matter for himself. He regarded himself and the other teachers as mere ministers employed by God in different parts of the one common work. The station assigned to each, the success granted to each, was determined by God. Whether as the layer of foundations, or the builder upon them; whether as a preacher to the Gentiles where the Gospel had never been carried before, or a presiding presbyter at Jerusalem; whether to fail and be driven off in one city, or to gain many converts in another; all these things alike were in the Divine counsels. What was best and wisest for the kingdom, he could not tell; but God who saw the end from the beginning could.

He would be only the soldier, to go whither he was sent, and to do what he was bidden. He would do earnestly and enthusiastically what he had to do. He would do it hopefully, also. He would know how to abound, when abundance came. But he would not be disheartened by failures, or let his fear of coming failure, which might indeed never come, disturb his trustfulness or his peace. His work was done to the best of his ability. What could he do more? The results must be committed to a higher wisdom and a mightier power than his own.

We, also, ought to be living in this way. It is a hard lesson for any of us to learn; but certainly, as the Apostle intimates, it is a peaceful one when it is learned. Take the case of your entrance upon the work of life, for example, or of a call to a particular service. You may be in some questioning as to the summons of duty. But if you determine this point as you best may, and then go forward, you may joyfully perform the labour of each day as it comes, and believe that all will be well at the end. And so in all your course. Like the daily bread which we are taught to ask for only for a single day, the daily duties are to occupy the thoughts. They come upon us clearly and plentifully enough, with each day as it passes. They bear with them the Divine voice, and the Divine summons. They are the private soldier's work. Why look beyond them to uncertain possibilities of the future, to bring a burden of distress upon the soul?

The Christian plan of living says to every man: Do what to-day calls for; fill it with everything which it asks; make such preparations for the future as the work which is under your care demands, and the probabilities of continued life suggest as wise. But be content when you have done this. Do not hinder the efficiency of to-day by anxiety for to-morrow. Do not make the uncertainty of results which you cannot control a burden upon your soul. That this plan is the right one for limited beings like ourselves can scarcely be doubted. That it is a reasonable one is certain, when we observe the facts of our earthly life. But, for *peacefulness*, it is the *only plan*. The man who makes it his rule to do the utmost that he can, and ought to do, to-day, and waits calmly for to-morrow, to follow the same course in its work, must be undisturbed. He must be in the line of the Divine appointment; and it is only because we forget this, that the worrying cares and fears that break in from the future destroy our happiness and our peace.

There is surely nothing grander than the words of the Apostle which have been quoted at the beginning of our discourse. There is nothing in human experience which seems to come forth more truly from, or testify more sweetly of, the peace of God that passeth all understanding. Filling each day with his duty as a preacher of the Gospel to all who would come to him, he was ready for whatever the Divine Master might send. To live would be for him, as he well knew, Christ; to die would be gain. He could scarcely determine which to choose. He was ready for either; and ready to leave the decision with the wisdom of that loving Friend who

84

had led him for so many years, and who had taught him, by many an experience, that the abounding and the abasing alike wrought out results of blessing at the end. Why should not the years have taught him to be anxious in nothing?

But, while the Christian disciple fulfils his appointed duty, leaving results with God, and thus, so far as he accords in his life with the doctrine, is free from anxiety that burdens the heart, he is not left with no manifestation of God, or communion with God. In everything, the Apostle adds, by prayer and supplication, with thanksgiving, let your requests be made known unto God. These words open before us a most delightful representation of Christian living. They show that, in the course of all His work and service, the Divine Father abides near the believer, and is ready to know and consider the wants, desires, and aspirations of his soul. They encourage him to present his thoughts and earnest wishes before God; and they allow and even direct him to let the range of his supplication extend itself to the whole circle of the things that interest his mind. The teaching of the New Testament is not, that we need not or should not be anxious for anything, because there is a destiny and fate which we cannot change — that we can only perform blindly the task which falls to us, there being no thought of us, or care for us, above ourselves. But it is, that we may make known our requests to a wiser Friend — laying before Him every pure thought, every plan and purpose and hope, every conception we have of what is best for the success of our working — that we have with Him the intercourse of a reverential fellowship ; — but only that, in the appreciation and acknowledgment of His wisdom as far greater than our own, we commit the decision to Him.

And this is to be in everything, and with giving of thanks. What is prayer, but the communing of the child with his father? It begins, indeed, in the earlier stages of the life, with simple petitions for the fundamental and necessary things. It asks for the first forgiveness, and the elementary teaching, and the tender care of the soul. But as the Christian grows into maturity, and his thoughts move through a wider circle, and his living becomes in all its parts a preparation for a greater life in another world, prayer rises into something higher. It is *then* the opening to God of what the mind is dwelling upon, and the meeting with Him in the meditation of the soul. As the child, in his later years, when he comes to the borders of manhood, enters into a new relation to his father, and there is a conferring of mind with mind on higher themes, so the disciple finds his thoughts going out towards God in every line. He lets the sanctifying influence of the Divine presence and communion rest upon all his inner life.

There is, thus, no limitation imposed with regard to any request which can find lodgment in a right thinking mind. But earthly and heavenly things alike are the proper subjects of our supplication; and where the man outside of the Christian sphere is filled with anxiety, the Christian is allowed to present his request for help or success, while the anxious feeling alone is put aside. We do not know, in our ordinary living, the full privilege of prayer; and therefore it loses for us, oftentimes, its richness and its blessing. But when we let it range throughout the whole circle of life, it makes God a personal present friend to us, — one to whom we can turn at any moment, and one through whom we can rise above the perplexities, and lose the anxious cares that press upon us.

Thus it is that thanksgiving naturally comes into the heart. The view of the true believer which the Apostle presents to us, is this: The man is placed in a condition where he cannot see the future. He is, however, appointed to a life which, in many ways, takes hold upon that future. He can realise it only as it comes, but he cannot fail to hope, or to plan for it. His mind reaches beyond its vision. What must he do? He must work as the duties open themselves, but he must leave the results. He must live the life of trust and faith. But, as he looks backward over what was a little while ago as uncertain as the coming time now is, he must observe the movement of the Divine plan and be thankful.

The call of the Christian teaching is to look behind us, as truly as it is to look before us. It is, indeed, to have our outlook upon the future wholly free from anxiety, as connected with the review of the way by which blessings have come to us in the past. No lesson of life is more universal in the experience of the disciples of Christ, than that the

overruling of God is always towards good. Those
things which for the present seem not to be joyous,
but grievous, work out afterwards the peaceable
fruits. The darkness of the days past has given
way to the light of to-day. It has how often, to
our own appreciation and knowledge now, been
itself the thing which has brought the light, and
been transformed into the light. And as we get
more fully the consciousness that life for each one
of us is God's plan of good, we may have confidence
that all this is so as truly in what we do not yet understand, as in what we do. Acknowledgment of
the goodness of God is, therefore, a part of every
true prayer ; and as we utter our thanksgiving, both
for what we have always known as blessings, and
for what we did not once realise to be such, but are
now understanding more completely, the gratitude
for the past brings with it a calm and loving com-
mittal of the future to Him who has guided us all
the way from the beginning.

And now the Apostle adds his word of assurance
and promise. If the soul moves on in this way —
in nothing allowing anxious care and fear to abide
within itself; in everything, with filial affection, and
with no doubtings as to the freeness of the offer,
making known its requests; in review of the past,
giving thanks for the working of all things together
for good, and in the outlook upon the future, asking
for what we desire, yet only realising that our desire
afterwards may be opposite to what it is now, when
we come to see the end — and thus ready to leave

the issues with Divine love and wisdom; — the declaration is, that the peace of God shall guard the heart and the thoughts in Christ Jesus. It requires no word from heaven, to assure us that there must be peacefulness in the soul when a man is living thus. But there is more than a simple assurance of peacefulness, in the Pauline sentence. The peace, it declares, will be the peace of God. The relation of the Christian soul to God, at the very beginning of the new life, involves as its chief element, or one of its chief elements certainly, a peculiar peacefulness. It is the peacefulness of reconciliation and reunion. The forgiveness of the past sins and the justification which accompanies it, as the Apostle says elsewhere, bring peace with themselves. But this is, as it were, the first experience, the first consciousness of the child-relationship to the Divine Father. With reference to what follows afterwards, it is but as the door which opens into the richer blessedness — the child's foretaste of what is to be realised in a measure, and with a fulness beyond present imagination, in the long-continued and growing manhood of the future years. The peace here described is that which God gives to the trusting soul in ever-enlarging measure, and which answers to His own peace. My peace, said Jesus to the disciples, I give unto you. Not as the world giveth, give I unto you. The peace of Jesus was that which belonged to Him and dwelt within Him, because of His union of love and purpose and inmost life with God. It was the peace which pertains to communion of souls, and its impartation

from one to the other is the result of the fellowship
of the two — the measure of the blessing being proportioned to the perfectness of the fellowship.

Into such fellowship the believer enters, who lives
after the manner which Paul sets forth. By his trustfulness, by his confidence in God which rises above
the power and the disturbing influence of anxiety,
by his prayer and supplication which go out into the
widest range of pure thought and desire, by his ever-
arising and ever-enduring thankfulness, he brings
his soul into that harmony with the Divine which
makes the gift of a peace like that of God Himself
possible for his experience. This peace, in its completeness in the Divine Father, is founded, as we
may believe, upon the two great truths, that He
abides in the light in which there is no darkness at
all, and is Himself this light, and that He also abides
in love, and is Himself love. The trustful soul does
not see all things and for this reason feel safe beyond all questionings. It does not have in itself the
perfection of the life of love. But it believes where
it does not yet see, and is moved to confidence and
steadfast hope by the love-power within itself; and
thus in the limitations of its knowledge it takes to
itself its measure of what God has and of what God
bestows. Its peace becomes like that of Jesus,
which dwelt in His soul always, and was, even in the
darkest hours, calm as the calmness of the ocean's
depths, because He knew the storms of life to be
under His Father's power, and therefore without the
ability to shake or disturb the trusting heart.

This peace it is, which the Apostle declares shall

be with the prayerful, grateful Christian, who lays aside his anxious fears and doubts.

But there is one peculiar word in the assurance set before us in the Pauline expression, which seems, in a sense, to involve the force of the promise. The peace of God, he says, shall guard your hearts and your thoughts. The figure is that of a city guarded from its enemies, or of a fortress, where the disciple is protected, as by an irresistible power, from all assaults from without. The thoughts and the whole sphere of the heart and mind will be kept secure from disturbing forces of uncertainty, or apprehension, or distress in view of the future. "Thou shalt keep him in perfect peace whose mind is stayed upon thee." The heavenly existence is begun already for the man who has truly and fully come into this peace, guarded by the Divine presence and guarding every thought in the sphere of Christ's own living. It is realised, in some measure, just as the soul enters into the trust that turns away anxiety and makes prayer and thankfulness the atmosphere of its life.

The years are steadily moving on, and they are rapidly passing away. What are they teaching us? More and more, surely, of the uncertainty of life ; more and more of the unsatisfactoriness of it, if there is nothing beyond. The men who were a little way before us, and who have suddenly passed within the region of the unseen, are testifying to us of what we are learning for ourselves — that the things of this world, good, and valuable, and worthy of thought as they may be, are only preparatory to something higher and future. The manly way of living, therefore, is not that of absorption in these things, as if these were all, but that of using them for what they may help us to attain. Life thus teaches us that they belong to a single and passing stage of our being, and that it is what they prepare us for in character and service, which gives them their true meaning. To be anxious for them in themselves, is like living for the day, and not for life. To be overburdened with trouble respecting what they may bring in the immediate future, is to forget that the temporary loss or trial in human experience often transforms itself into glorious blessing. It is to make the future subordinate to the present, for we lose sight of what the present may do for the future, and lose care for it.

I cannot but think that, as life moves on, the man who lives aright sees more clearly that he is in a process of education, and understands more fully that he is dependent for wisdom and guidance on a higher power. We know, in the retirement of our own souls, that we are limited, weak, and ignorant beings, whose knowledge and vision reach but a little way. How can peace come to us, except through committing our way to the Divine Father, and losing our anxiety in prayer to Him for the future, and grateful feeling for the past?

The Apostle to the Gentiles had a manly soul, if any one ever had. He was earnest in labour; ardent in feeling; enthusiastic as a youth, through all his life; intensely full of energy for the completion of his work before the end; hopeful for the future, and burning with desire that it should bring triumph to the cause. But he died while the victory was still in the distant and unseen coming age; yet he had no doubts; no cloud gathered over his spirit; no weariness made him ready to lay down his work in despair, for another to take it. He finished his course with the same confidence with which he had passed through it. He went away from the peace of earth, as his soul had experienced it in Jesus Christ, to the peace of heaven. But it was here, as it was to be there, a peace that had no anxious forebodings — the peace which passes all understanding —the peace of God, which kept his heart and guarded every thought. A grand living and a grand dying — like that of the Master Himself. What a blessedness for us, if it may be ours also! The lesson is a Divine one, full of love; — but it is a difficult one to learn. I commend it to all others, and to myself.

VII

THE TRUE LIFE OF MAN NOT IN HIS POSSESSIONS

A man's life consisteth not in the abundance of the things which he possesseth. — LUKE xii. 15.

THIS sentence is also translated, and perhaps more properly: A man's life, even if he have abundance, does not consist in what he possesses. In either case — only that there is a certain greater emphasis with the latter rendering — the declaration is the same : — that life is not to be found in what a man has, however abundant what he has may be, but in something independent of this.

One of the multitude accompanying Jesus at the time, and listening to His teachings, said to Him : Master, bid my brother divide the inheritance with me. Jesus reminded him, in answer to his request, that it was not a part of His mission in the world as the Christ to pass judicial decisions in such matters, and then, perceiving the motive which had impelled the man in his demand, He turned to the people about Him, and addressed to them these words : Do not be ever desiring and striving to have more than you already have. The gaining of more does not bring you life. Even if you gain more, and

94

much more — up to the limits of great abundance — life, in case you then have it, will not consist in what you have gained. Life is something deeper and more personal than this. It is, like the kingdom of God itself, not around you, but within you.

This is the Christian doctrine concerning life, and it is in accordance with all analogies, and with all that we know. Among the questions of these recent days, one which awakens greatest interest is, What is life? The search which is pressed further than all other searchings is that which seeks to discover it. We would lay our hands upon life, and determine its nature and its essence. It eludes our grasp, indeed, and leaves us in disputation. We are compelled to wait for the future to answer our questioning, or to acknowledge the possibility that no answer may ever be given. But however we may divide in our thoughts about it, or whatever may be the measure of our knowledge or fancied knowledge, there is one thing revealed to us the more clearly and impressively, the further we carry forward our investigations. This one thing is told us, each and all alike. It is, that life lies back of anything which we have yet discovered. We know life's acquisitions, its activities, its varied revelations of itself. But it is not itself these, or in these alone. It has a being of its own, and moves and gains by its own vital force. The movement is not *itself*. It is the outreaching of its energy towards and after that which will minister to its growth, or enjoyment, or well-being. But the life precedes the motion. The

95

gains, also, are not the life. They are additions to it, in one form or another — sometimes near its inmost self, far more often quite outside of it, and never, and nowhere, of its own primal and independent essence. Life by its living power gains for, or even in, itself; but its existence is the condition of the forthputting of the power which gains. It is the source of the power, as well as of that which the power secures.

All this is true, moreover, not only in the physical sphere, within which the questioning is so often and so urgently raised, but in every sphere. The essence of the intellectual life of the student, in any department of learning, is not to be found in that which he brings into his mind by his studies, or in the act of his studying. These things are the results of the life. They are the evidences of its existence, it may be. But they are not the life itself. Let a man examine himself, and he may know this. You and I, if we enter into the realisation of our souls' deepest experience, do not rejoice as men of living minds in what we have acquired of learning or knowledge, within the last week or the last year, as if this were the most joyful thing. We rejoice in the living mind which acquired for itself the knowledge of the past time, and which may acquire for itself far different knowledge, and far more, in the future time. However abundant the acquisitions may be, we know that they are added to ourselves — possessions which we have gained — things which we have made our own. But the thing which is gained is not a blessing like the thing by which it is gained. The former may pass away perchance, or may lose itself in what is greater and comes afterward, or may prove itself to be almost useless at times. But the latter is ever-abiding. It is a power through whose energy losses may be repaired, new and ever-enlarging acquirements may be brought into the possession of the life, the development even of itself may become continually greater. The knowledge which the mind possesses is one thing. The knowing mind is another and far better thing. It is better and grander, because it can gather into itself all the possibilities of the other; and because *the life* is in it, and not in the other. The central blessing which we have as educated men, is the intellectual life. Forth from this centre moves every energy which fills the life with its possessions.

The moral and spiritual life follows, as it were, the same law of our being. It is to be discovered, if discovered at all, in the deep recesses of the man, far away from and below all external things. It is the breath of God, which is breathed into the man as he first enters upon the sphere where these things have their being. It is the inspiration of the Divine nature within him, by which he is made fit for a purer and higher atmosphere than that of the evil and passing world. It is most truly a life from above, imparted to him and implanted within him. It must therefore, in a pre-eminent degree, be an energising force, which gains great things for itself, but which is independent of these things. They are what it has. It is what it is. They are the fruits which it puts forth — the possessions which it

7   97

places, it may be, in closest relation to itself, and uses for its own development — the glorious manifestion of what it contains within itself, perchance, and thus the revealing of itself to the eye that sees. But it is the God-given principle — the power that worketh all things.

But if life, in any department of our being, is not to be discovered in what it gains for itself, much less even, it would seem, can life in one department consist in the possessions secured by life in another department. The intellectual life, surely, cannot have its being in that which the physical life acquires by the forthputting of its peculiar powers. It must move in its own sphere, and reach out after what may satisfy its own desires. The forces of the two lives work along different lines. They may indeed co-operate with each other, in some degree, so that the gains of the former may be larger by reason of what the latter has done for itself. But if this be the fact in any case, the things which the one life is partly enabled to secure through the aid of the other are essentially unlike anything which that other knows as its own possession. The rewards of the mind belong within the sphere of mental effort and working, and this sphere is not that of the physical powers, even when these, by reason of the mysterious union of body and mind, may quicken or strengthen the mental effort. Indeed, so true is this, that we often find the one life active while the other is not, or the energy which is put forth in the line of the one so exclu-

98

sively taking possession of the man, as it were, that there is a corresponding loss of power in the line of the other. One of the great difficulties in every man's work for himself is to adjust the two in their mutual relations, and thus to guard successfully against the danger of losing the life in one sense, while it is saved in another. This, indeed, is a problem of chief importance in all education — a problem in connection with which the successes and failures alike show the one truth, that each life must gain for itself, and cannot consist in, or depend upon, what the other gains.

We may compare the spiritual life, again, with either of the other two, and the truth will manifest itself, only if possible the more clearly. The spiritual life is character. Its gains are gains in virtue, and purity, and the development of all goodness. How can its living force be found in knowledge, or physical strength or beauty, or in anything which may be secured for the man without building up the moral part of him?

The story in the Gospel from which our verse is taken may reveal the fact to us. Jesus was speaking of the spiritual life, when He used these words. The man who had come to Him — with the strange request, as it would seem, to be made of such a teacher — was thinking of the inheritance which pertained to his family. It was houses and lands and goods of every sort — possessions, in the sense in which we use the word in our ordinary conversation — that he was thinking of and asking for. An abundance greater than what he at present had

was the object which he desired; and seeing plainly
where it was, and how it might be at once secured,
he presented the case to Jesus for His aid. What
were his thoughts respecting life? They were certainly thoughts concerning it as moving, and having
its being, in one sphere only — that of the abundance of the things possessed through the inheritance of an estate. But how could it be possible to
discover the life which Jesus thought of simply in
such abundance? The things which made up the
inheritance had been acquired by the powers of
another sort of life than this. They were independent of it, and it was independent of them. They
might pass into the possession of the man without
touching the character, whether for good or for
evil. They might even impoverish the character,
while they enlarged the estate. It is evident,
indeed, that in the case of this man such impover-
ishment was the result which was distinctly foreseen.
The life, therefore, could not consist in the abundance of the possessions. It might, perchance,
co-exist with such abundance, even for this man,
if he would take into himself the true idea, and live
by it; but, whether he should do so or not, it could
not consist in it. It could not, because the life and
the abundance were widely and essentially separate
from each other. The abundance was an acquire-
ment of the mental or physical life, or both together; but the life now thought of was spiritual,
and pertained to the soul. The life of the soul,
surely, the central part of the man, cannot be the
external possessions of a less central life. It cannot

depend on houses, and lands, and rich inheritance, and the right sharing of ancestral property. It lies back even of what it gains for itself by the exercise of its own powers. Surely, it must lie far away from what is gained by powers other than its own, and from that abundance of which it knows nothing and thinks nothing within its own sphere.

For this reason it was, that Jesus said to the people who were standing by Him: Keep yourselves carefully from the overweening, all-controlling desire for abundance of possessions. The thing to be desired, with the all-controlling movement of the soul, is life. Take heed — the life is in one place, the abundance in another; and when the desire for the abundance becomes an inordinate desire, the life is lost. How true His words are to human experience — and how true they are also, when He points forward to the future and gives another reason why the life does not consist in the possessions. The little illustrative story that follows tells of the ending of the one, and the continuance of the other. The life moves onward, and the abundance falls away. The gain which the powers have secured in one department of the man's living is a treasure which may be lost for him in a day. The ever-living life of the man, certainly, must be independent of this, and must be separate and distinct from it, however abundant it may be.

This indeed it is, which glorifies us as men. We are ourselves, in every line, greater and deeper than anything that we have gained outside of ourselves. We live, and the gains pass away or are forgotten.

They pass away because of the earth and time, or they are forgotten by reason of the far greater ones that we make for ourselves afterwards. But we move on, with living power, beyond them and above them. The life of to-day, for each one of us, is not found in the abundance which we secured ten years ago. No more is it in that which we now possess. The abundance is dying, it may be, but we are living. The abundance is of this world, but we are taking hold in our life upon what is higher than this world. The immortal part cannot consist in the mortal part. Most truly it cannot have its life in what the mortal part only possesses.

These thoughts are clear to us, so soon as we give them a lodgment in our minds. They seem so plain, perhaps, as scarcely to need any expression. Of course, we are prompted to say, Of course, life is different from the gains of life, and life in one sphere cannot be made out of the acquisitions of life in another sphere. But how many are there in any company of men who bear within themselves the thought — and give it a practical realisation in their daily thinking — that they are *themselves* more than all that they are *doing*, or *gaining*, or *making their own*, and that their life is *behind and beneath all these things?* The mass of men about us are like the man who came, at this time, to Jesus. They are pressing after the possessions — seeking after the inheritance — struggling for a division of it — striving everywhere for more. It is *the additions* to the life, which fill their minds and impel their efforts. Happiness is to be found in these additions, for it is these which give comfort and restfulness and freedom from all burdens, it is said: One may well sacrifice all else for these, and put forth the labour of years to secure them. Perhaps no age in the world's history has been more full of such thoughts than the one which is now opening upon us. This influence is working rapidly into the minds of educated men, and they are beginning everywhere to feel that life needs more of what is external, if its perfect ideal is to be attained. Even the student moves after wealth as one of the greatest things — or if perhaps not after this, after station, and comfortable place, and large fame, as if these were the main ends of living. Everything centres, as it were, in what one has; and so the desire to have more lays ever stronger hold upon the soul.

The message which comes over the ages to us, in the midst of our thinking, is the word which came to this man. The life is not in the possessions. It is elsewhere. It is no more in them when they are abundant, than it is when they are scanty. It has, so far as its essence and central forces are concerned, nothing to do with them. It may use them, but they are not itself. It may enjoy what they may enable it to secure, but it may have its true enjoyment without them, as well as with them. It is, in the widest and deepest meaning of the expression, *one thing*, while they are *another*.

To educated men this message may have an

especial emphasis, for their own experience may tell them somewhat of its truth. The true student knows, when he comes to himself in his thinking, that his peculiar life is within, not without himself — that he is independent of lands and houses and the external gifts for which so many seek — that the treasure of his mind and soul is the treasure of knowledge and thought. He may live anywhere, and this treasure abides with him. He may share the inheritance and gain the abundance, or not, and the essential life is the same. But even the educated man may lose the power of the lesson. The Christian teaching is needed for him, as it is needed for all, while it utters its voice concerning a life deeper than his, as it is also deeper than that of those who live wholly in the outward possessions. The life is the central thing in the man. It is what makes the man in his manhood; — not in his learning, not in his inheritance, not in his wealth, but in his *manhood.* And the *manhood alone* is *the essence of the man.* This is what Jesus taught the people. This is the great truth of the matter. Take heed, He says, and do not forget it. Keep yourselves from the ever-continuing desire for more, as if in the possessing of more the secret of the life were to be discovered.

My friend, you are, perchance, preparing in your earlier years for the future — for your own future. You believe in that future; you anticipate it joyfully and hopefully; you feel, in your most thoughtful moments, that it is far better and far more than the present, and that your life is in it. What is the end in view of your preparation? Is it to *be some-thing*, or to *have something*? If the primary object is, to have something, your years and efforts will be given to gaining possessions of one kind or another. Your desires will continually be for more, and the result, if you are successful, will be additions to yourself — additions in the outward sphere, and in the field of the abundance of which Jesus was speaking. But you will be working away from the centre, and may be losing, daily, more and more of that which abides there. The inheritance of the man in the story would have been secured to him, we may believe, if Jesus had yielded to his request and bidden the brother give him his rightful portion. He would have lived on his estate, and stored his possessions, and laid up his treasure ever more abundantly for himself, and found the wishes of the early days fulfilled. But the abundance would have been around him, not within him. Within him, if we may listen to the suggestion of the narrative, would have been one of the baser of the passions — and constantly increasing in its strength — the un-satisfied desire for more; covetousness, as the Scriptural word describes it. The outward things would have been growing, but the inward things — so far as they were worthy of a noble manhood — would have been steadily diminishing and dying away, while, in place of them, would have been rising into being and victorious power evil affections and impulses destructive of the true life. The living in the one sphere would have been attended by the dying in the other, and the manhood of the man would have been gradually ruined and lost.

There are men of the highest positions in the world, at this moment — strange to say, there are men whose educated life should, by its most impressive lessons, be giving them a nobler inspiration — of whom this melancholy truth is as true as it was, or could have been, of the man in the Gospel story. Their manhood is perishing, while their fame or wealth is growing. The inward life is dying, while the outward life is continually gathering more into its forces and its gifts. But the man comes to himself now and again, in some serious hour of self-contemplation, or he will come to himself in the future, — and then he knows, or will know, where the life is — not in the abundance, but in the manhood. If the manhood is gone, the abundance has no vital source beneath it. The things possessed are worthless when the possessor is nothing.

But, with the life in its living force, the man is triumphant. He finds in every place enough of duty and service for the exercise of all his powers. He finds in himself an ever-springing fountain of thought and love. He sees the divinely-implanted seed growing within him, and yielding its fruit day by day. He knows himself to be what he ought to be — not all that he ought to be, perchance, or all that he hopes to be, but moving towards it; — living within himself, and therefore to live always.

How fitting it seems that, just after this story and the parable that accompanies it, the evangelist should place the words which Jesus addressed to the disciples: Therefore I say unto you, Be not anxious for your life, what ye shall eat; nor yet for your body, what ye shall put on. For the life is more than the food, and the body than the raiment. Seek ye God's kingdom and His righteousness, and these things shall be added unto you. Where your treasure is, there will your heart be also. Fear not, little flock; it is your Father's good pleasure to give you the kingdom.

It is the kingdom for which we should ever be preparing, for the abundance of the life itself is there. All else is an addition, but the life is the man. All else may pass away, but the life moves on to the greater life beyond. All else may be laid aside or forgotten, without a permanent loss to the soul, but the life is yourself. Take heed, says the Master, the life is not in the world; it is more than the world. It is infinitely better to gain it, than to gain the world. It is infinitely sad to lose it, for it is the loss of the man.

VIII

THE FOLLOWING OF CHRIST

Follow me. — JOHN i. 43.

[The entire verse reads as follows: *On the morrow he was minded to go forth into Galilee, and he findeth Philip: and Jesus saith unto him, Follow me.*]

THE passage from which these words are taken as the subject of our thought is the first one in the order of the biographical record of the career of Jesus, in which they are found. We meet them, however, in six other places, as we move forward in our reading of the Gospel story from its beginning towards its ending, and we find them unfolding their meaning to us as they are spoken on different occasions and are addressed to different persons. They involve the one central demand and call of the Christian life — the words remaining always the same; — but they suggest more and more of the detail of duty, and indicate the varied applications of the call, when the several narratives in which they occur are gathered together in one, as it were, and they are viewed in comparison with each other.

To the young ruler who asked Him what he should do to inherit eternal life, Jesus said, Go, sell that thou hast, and give to the poor, and thou shalt have treasure in heaven: and come, follow me. To the man who proposed to begin his service and discipleship, but asked for delay that he might first go and bury his father, the answer was, Follow me; and leave the dead to bury their own dead. To Matthew, who was in the ordinary business of his life as a tax-gatherer, the sudden and abrupt summons came — possibly without any previous intimation of such a change — to leave his occupation, and be a new man in a new work. Jesus saw him sitting at the place of toll, says the evangelist, and said unto him, Follow me; and he arose and followed him. Philip, whom John mentions in the verse selected for our text, was found by Jesus, perhaps accidentally, and was asked to join the two disciples who had met Him on the day before, and to accompany Him on His return to Galilee. *Follow me* was to him, as to them, an invitation to form the acquaintance of Jesus, and to come under those influences which might lead to faith and discipleship. Peter and Andrew, James and John, two of whom, and perhaps all of whom, had thus been summoned to acquaintanceship, and to the friendly study of Jesus' character and claims, in the earlier days, were afterwards, by the same words, Follow me, bidden to enter upon the Apostolic office, and become permanent associates of the Master, whom they had already learned to love, in His proclamation of the kingdom. One of these four — the leader of them all — heard the bidding once more, when the ministry of Jesus had come to its end and the rising from the dead had given its witness to His power. The Lord told him of what was awaiting him in the future, and of the manner of his death, and then said to him, Follow me — words which were repeated, a few moments afterward, in answer to his question with respect to John's coming experience and destiny: If I will that he tarry till I come, what is that to thee? Follow thou me.

Finally, we discover the same call and bidding in that last prophetic utterance of Jesus, when He was reminded, by the desire of certain Greeks to see Him, and talk with Him, of the universal triumph of His kingdom. Turning the thought of Andrew and Philip, the very disciples whom He had met on the first two days of His working, to the great fundamental principle of self-sacrifice, He uttered the comprehensive sentence, applicable to all who would hear His voice, If any man serve me, let him follow me. These are the several recorded instances in which the words were used. What may we say of the words, as we review them?

We say of them: The same and yet not the same. The word meant to one a sacrifice at the central and inmost point of his soul's life — the consent to part with his great possessions for the good of the poor, and thus the contradiction of his deepest affections and desires, in order that he might gain even the first entrance into the life of which he had been thinking. No following was possible for such as he, unless the man was changed in that secret region of his character which, as yet, he had not opened to his own view, and into which he did not wish to look, even for a moment. To another, who thought himself a disciple and declared himself ready to act accordingly, only with an excuse for a temporary delay, the meaning was, the *immediateness* of the call of duty. No excuse can defer the first and foremost obligation of life. Natural affection is, indeed, a beautiful thing, and the love of parents is no less truly a Divine command, than it is a pure and noble impulse of the heart. But even the demands which come from this must not hinder the response of the soul to a voice from the Divine Father, who claims the supreme place for Himself. Let the spiritually dead take care of the burial of the physically dead — leave them alone to do this — is a word which may not need to be often spoken; for the life of discipleship moves ordinarily along the lines of the common earthly loves and duties. But there are times when it carries with it the summons of the only true life, and when — by the startling emphasis with which it bids us neglect, and leave behind us, that service of the family and of dearest friendships which, as we are wont to say, glorifies our manhood — it teaches the solemn lesson that character cannot wait, and that the turning of the soul towards the right which, for any reason, is put off to a later season, is no true turning at all. Character lies not in a coming time, but in the present. Life belongs to to-day, and the reformation or renewal which we only propose to ourselves for to-morrow is far more uncertain than is to-morrow itself.

But, on the other hand, the significance of the

words as they were uttered to Philip, in the text, and
to Andrew and his friend, on the previous day, was
all in the line of gentleness. We would know where
you are abiding, they said to Jesus, in order that we
may speak with you in confidence of the great things
for which we are waiting in the kingdom of God, and
may know also something of yourself. Come and
see; follow me; was the answer. Come with me,
and let us talk together; and suffer the impressions
of what you see and hear to-day, and to-morrow, and
the day following, to take their rightful hold upon
your souls, as you would in the intercourse of any
friendship. I ask nothing more of you now. When
I say, *Follow me*, to honest, earnest men like you, I
mean live for a season in a nearness of mind and
heart to me, according to the laws and nature of a
friendly union, and then test the matter by your own
experience and form your decision. I have no fears
for the result; and you will not have, I am sure,
two or three days hence. Only follow me naturally,
easily, not suspiciously, not demanding more than I
do, for these days. This was His meaning. They
yielded to His reasonable demand, and the forces of
the new life were implanted in their hearts.

Then, after the few days had passed, He suffered
them — we may believe that He even urged them —
to return to their homes and their occupations again.
There — by the lake-side, and in their daily round of
homely duties — they were to let the impulse and
spirit, which they had gained in their brief union
with Him, work out into action and life quietly, while
they had no thought of greater things for themselves,

until the new teaching of the new friend should
manifest itself as the truth by reason of its recognised
power within their souls. The character was to
grow gently and easily — even as the living seed had
been so naturally and tenderly planted at the first —
until it should be ripened and strengthened enough
for the Master's use. This was the plan and the
movement, as we see by the story; and, after a
season, Jesus called them again.

But when the call came again, with its repetition
of the same words which they had heard before,
what a depth and breadth of meaning it carried in
itself! It meant now a life-long service, with all of
self-denial and labour and persecution, and with all
of joy also and courage and victory, which it might
involve. They were prepared to understand it now
— that it signified a giving up of all that they had
known and done in their past experience, for His
sake ; — and they were ever ready to yield obedience
to the summons. They heard the familiar words,
uttered by the voice which they knew, and in a
moment, without a hesitating thought, they left their
boats, and their father, to follow Him for all the
future. The decisive step which should never be
recalled, was taken immediately. But, because of
the quiet preparation and the time allowed for it,
it was taken as naturally as the step which turned
their course towards the house where He was temporarily abiding, when He said to them, Come and
see.

Thus it was in all the cases. The suddenness of
the call to Matthew, if indeed it was as sudden and

unexpected as it appears in the story to have been, and the instantaneousness of his answering act, bore evidence of something, in his life and thought, which filled the words for him with a controlling force and energy for the will. There have been lives since the Apostolic age, in every generation, in which such calls, at a critical moment, have been the first and effective summons to a permanently changed career. The significance of the call was appreciated by the man himself; the result only, which seemed perchance to have been without a cause proportioned to its greatness, was visible to others. But with most men, it is not so. They move along the more even paths; and, if they hear the Christian call at all, they reason according to the way which Jesus Himself pointed out in His more general word: If any man serve me, let him follow me. If I enter the service of any master who calls for the exercise of the true life-powers of the soul, it becomes me to obey his voice as it utters the command *follow me;* and as a genuine man, worthy of the name, I will do that which alone befits the life which I have chosen. The reasoning which they thus carry forward in their minds abides with them. It affects their living gradually, yet constantly and powerfully, and they become, as time passes on, thoughtful and earnest followers of him whom they serve.

The summons which these words bear with them thus had in the Gospel stories a special significance in each several case — and we may believe that it was so, also, in the many instances in Jesus' lifetime where He gave utterance to the bidding *follow me,* but which have not been recorded for our reading by the evangelists. The call to all alike was one, but its meaning varied with the circumstances and peculiarities of each individual case. As we have said at the outset, The same, and yet not the same.

But with equal fitness, and in accordance with what the several narratives suggest to us, we may turn our expression into its opposite in order and in thought, and say: Not the same, and yet the same. And the full presentation of what the words contain will not be brought before us, until we view the summons in this light also.

The words involved, first of all — in every case — decision and promptness of action. We may observe this most clearly in the story of the man who wished to wait until he had fulfilled the office of natural affection in the burial of his dead father, and in the call to the young ruler to give up for the help of others the wealth which was the dearest possession of his soul. Decision was essential, in these cases, at the moment and in preparation for the first step in the life of discipleship. So, on the other side, it was evidently essential, when the call came to Matthew, at the receipt of toll, or to Andrew and John, at the sea of Galilee. The immediateness of the decision, which these men made, was manifest in what they did. Without a thought or a question, they rose and left all. They formed in a moment the determination of a life-time. The brief record of this call to Matthew which the evangelist gives, and the single sentence wherein he sums up the action on which all the future depended, have arrested and impressed the mind of every thoughtful reader from the writer's day to ours.

But these were not the only cases. The same promptness of decision was involved in the simple invitation which was given, on the first day, to the two young disciples of John the Baptist. By reason of their condition, and of the end which both they and Jesus had in view, the change of character was not centred so wholly, and so apparently, in the one act, as it was in the cases previously mentioned. But the one act here, as elsewhere, was nevertheless the first essential thing. The consent to follow Jesus to His lodging, or to Galilee, was that which opened the mind and heart, instead of closing them. The life-movement afterward was in the new direction, and towards the light and truth of the kingdom, because the footsteps were turned, at that hour, into the way along which the words of Jesus called them. If the men had lingered for a while doubting, or had refused to obey the call, the opportunity might have passed, and the life might never have grown into faith and discipleship. And we may easily believe that those who had been slow to be trustful and to act, at that moment, would not have received, at a later season, the summons to the service and glory of the Apostolic office. The greater calls of the future, in all our living, follow along the line of the lesser ones of the past and the present, and the man who refuses a decision for right character as the gateway towards the attainment of it opens, may find the path beyond the gateway closed to his life.

The words of Jesus may come to us, in many ways, bidding us follow Him. They may have their own significance for each one of us, because of something which is individual and peculiar to our lives. But however they come and whatever may be their special meaning, they call for prompt decision somewhere; and this prompt decision is vitally connected with character, and lies near the sources and foundation of the inner life.

The words of the call of Jesus involved also, in every case, a personal relation to Him. Philip was invited to follow Him, that he might grow into the friendship of Jesus and grow into friendship towards Him. So it was, even pre-eminently, when the two pairs of brothers were called away from their friends and their business, at the sea of Galilee, and bidden to be fishers of men as preachers of the Gospel. So it was, also, at the end, when Peter was told of his own future and his martyrdom. *Follow me* meant to him that, in his coming years, he should live, in the soul's life, in union with the Friend who was now to be removed from his bodily sight and presence, and, in loving service and work for Him, should triumph over the thought of the trial before him, and even glory in it.

So it was everywhere. Following after Jesus was never presented in His teaching as a mere imitation of His example, or obedience to His commands. It had a significance far deeper than this; and, by

reason of this deeper significance, the teaching set
itself apart from every other doctrine and system.
It meant the personal union of the disciple with the
Master — a communion between the souls of the
two, kindred to that between the souls of loving men
— as real and vital as such human communion, and
laying hold even more powerfully upon the inmost
spirit. This is of the essence of Christianity. It
is its central truth, so far as life and experience are
concerned. The Christian call, whenever it comes
to us, is to the attainment of this. Its promise is
the promise of the realisation of what it tells us of
and offers to us. Why should not wealth and
earthly good be sacrificed for the union of the soul
with the Divine? Why should not the privilege and
duty of earthly affection be set aside, when the
heavenly friendship opens itself to our personal experience? Why should not the cross itself be taken
up by any man, when it is found in the pathway
which leads toward that following after Christ which
is communion and fellowship and friendship with
Him? The Gospel stories place these questions
before us, as we pass from one of them to another,
and they bear with them their answer. To follow
Jesus means to be united with Him, in such a
union that His life becomes the disciple's life, and
the two are, at the end, one — even with that oneness which unites the Father and the Son in love.

The words of the call, we may say once more, involved a complete consecration to the work of the
Master. Christian character grows indeed, like

all character. Christian principle develops and strengthens in its power and energy. The full fruits we see at the end, not at the beginning. But who can fail to observe, as he studies carefully the New Testament narratives, that the young ruler's selling his property, or Philip's consenting to accompany Jesus — different as the one act was from the other — was a first and decisive step towards that fulness of devotion to which Jesus pointed the thought of Peter, when He gave him, as His final, personal word, the bidding to put aside all care as to the manner of his own dying, and all questioning as to allotments of life for his nearest friend, and to concentrate his whole mind and soul and spirit on one thing — the following after Christ. And then, if we turn from the history to the letters of this Apostle, and his friend also, about whom he asked his question, and find *the men revealed* in what they wrote long years after the ending of Jesus' life, how clearly we see that the growth and fruitage of the last days were only the development of that which was planted in their souls when they first listened to the words *follow me.*

It was the same thing from the beginning to the ending. The devotion of the life to the Apostolic work, when the call was given at the Galilean lakeside, was in itself but one manifestation of the spirit which the call involved. The act and course to which it moved the four disciples pertained to their peculiar work and duty. But it was illustrative of the spirit involved in *every call,* in which the words *follow me* came from the lips of Jesus. The im-

mediateness and, as we may say, comprehensiveness
of the act on their part strikingly exhibit the distinctive feature of all obedience to such a summons,
which in and of itself, means the absolute and complete turning of the character at the outset, and its
full development at the end.

And so the call comes down the centuries, from
those early days to ours — the same, yet not the
same; or, on the other side, though not the same,
yet indeed one and the same. It meets us now, as
we ask where we shall find Jesus, and what we shall
find in Him — the question which Andrew and Philip
asked. It meets us again, when we inquire the way
to eternal life; or propose to enter into discipleship
when the earthly calls are satisfied; or think of our
future hopes and possibilities; or see the crosses
which life brings to all of us; or raise the question
of life's permanent work and duty. But everywhere
it sounds in our hearing the words *follow me*, and
tells us the meaning of those words: — that their
meaning is service, as to a Divine Friend — that it
is yielding to His influence, and knowing His friendship — that it is the immediate devotion of our souls
to Him, and the receiving into our souls the principles and powers of the true life, which shall develop
into strength and beauty of Christ-like character
through all the future.

IX

OUR CITIZENSHIP IN HEAVEN

For our citizenship is in heaven. — PHILIPPIANS iii. 20.

THE prominent word which Paul uses in this sentence is derived from the Greek noun denoting a citizen, or member of a city or state. Its precise significance as here employed has been a matter of some discussion — particularly as to the question whether it should be rendered in our language by the word *citizenship*, as given in the text of the Revised English Version, or *commonwealth*, as the margin of that version reads. In either case, the Apostle applies to the condition and life of the believer in Christ a term which involved the idea of membership in a state, and especially in a free state, with the privileges and rights pertaining to such membership. The other word which he uses marks the locality of this state, and thus indicates the character of the citizenship. The commonwealth to which the Christian belongs is the heavenly, and not an earthly one. He is a free citizen of this commonwealth; and, as the Apostle views his condition, the privileges and membership are his now, for he joins the words of his sentence by the present tense of a strong verb: Our citizenship is — our commonwealth subsists, and has a real, and objective, and present existence, in heaven. The fact, however, that it is in heaven, while the believer is yet on earth, and the intimation given in the latter part of the verse of a waiting for a future event — the coming of the Lord Jesus — which alone is to bring the complete realisation of the blessing, show that, according to the thought of the writer, the citizenship is viewed in its relation to one who is, for a time, absent from the home city and sojourning elsewhere. The believer is not in heaven, but the citizenship, the commonwealth to which he belongs, is there. The close connection of the words, finally, with those which precede and follow, indicate the bearing of this thought of citizenship, as the Apostle desired to present it to his readers. The sentence begins with the word *for*, and, through it, points backward to a context suggestive of *duties ;* and it passes, at its ending, into words referring to heaven and what shall be accomplished in the future, and thus turns the mind to *privileges* and *hopes*.

Such is the text. I present it for consideration, for a little time, as we view it in this light. What is the privilege; and what is the hope; and what is the duty, involved for the Christian in his membership in the heavenly commonwealth, while he is on earth?

We may consider it, first, with respect to privilege. It is evident that the citizen of any state, when absent from his home and resident in a foreign land, cannot be in the full exercise and enjoyment of the privileges which appertain to him as a citizen. Limitations, in this regard, are connected necessarily with his present condition, and so there is a sphere for patient waiting and for hope of a larger and better future. It is evident, also, that these limitations may check or hinder, for a time, the development of the life and character along the lines of these privileges. We grow, as we enjoy, where the conditions of our life are perfectly fitted for its growth. Where the conditions are not thus fitted, the powers may become weaker, or they may work toward loss and failure. But the man who has that within himself which his birthright in the state has made his own will bear it with him everywhere, and, notwithstanding the limitations, will be conscious of its presence as a privilege and a power.

The first element in this privilege is *the life-principle* of the commonwealth — that which is central to its own being. The citizen of the free commonwealth knows within himself such a life-principle of freedom, which makes him a different man from the men of the foreign land where he may be temporarily abiding, and as he knows it, he knows also the blessing which belongs to him in consequence of its indwelling power. The fundamental idea on which the constitution and organisation of the state are based has become, by reason of his citizenship, the foundation of his own character. The manhood in him takes hold upon this idea and principle, and in all its development makes itself strong by reason of its hold upon them. The Christian believer has a possession of a kindred sort. He does not yet realise the full privileges of the heavenly commonwealth, but he has powers and gifts which come forth from it. The laws and principles of the commonwealth work upon and into his personality, and make him a new man. The fundamental idea of this commonwealth is righteousness — a righteousness which is based upon love and enters into the heart as a living reality through faith. Its laws are directed to this end. Its principles find their centre and source of being in this. This righteousness is secured to him from the moment of his spiritual birth, and is the atmosphere of the life to which he is born, as truly as is liberty in the case of one who, by his birthright, is a member of the civil state that is established for freedom. Having once entered his life, it never leaves him. It only grows in its strength as time moves forward.

The privilege of the citizenship is here. I am not, indeed, perfect in the development of my life as yet; I am subject to the assaults of temptation, and am so weak in my powers until now, and so involved in the evils of the world in which I am living, that I sometimes or oftentimes fall, under the force of these assaults, into wrong-doing and sin. My actions belong, as they seem, to the commonwealth in which I have my dwelling-place for a season, rather than to that which claims me for itself, and to which I am hoping to take my way. But this is the weakness which comes from absence from my home and its surroundings, and from the forgetfulness, for the time, of the great principles of the life of my own commonwealth. When I come back to myself, and look into the deeper recesses of my soul for the life-power which is central to my spiritual

being, I find that it is still that which made its
entrance within me, at the beginning, from heaven,
and secured to me the citizenship of the heavenly
state. And so I rejoice in my birthright, and try to
live up to it. And so I take heart for the new conflict with temptation, and, peradventure, I win a victory, where I lost one before. And so I see that
the vital force becomes stronger and more all-controlling — gradually, it may be, but surely — as my
course moves onward, and the citizenship bears new
witness continually for itself. This is the Christian
career. It is privilege and possession at the beginning, and not merely at the end. It is, under whatever figure we may represent it, reality to-day,
though, with reference to its fulness, it may be
realisation only hereafter. It is therefore, as we use
the figure now before us, a citizenship whose life-
principle for the inner life is present with its transforming and ennobling energy when we are in the
foreign land, and whose promise is ever laying hold
upon the future.

But the privilege of the citizen is not merely in
the fundamental principle of the commonwealth. It
is found also in the influence of the life of the membership. We do not, as we grow up into the possession of the freedom of the civil state, gain the
privilege of our citizenship through the working of
liberty in our individual lives only. This is but
half of what is accomplished for us. The fact that
we do not breathe the atmosphere *alone*, is as important to our attaining the full results, as that we
breathe it *at all*. No man liveth for himself or by

himself, in any sphere of the inner life, who lives for the best ends. He draws from the common life, and becomes greater and better by receiving into himself the lessons, and influences, given forth from the growths of character, which are manifest in the large and noble and pure-minded men around him, who have been taught by the same masters or have been impelled by the same forces.

It is thus, even in a peculiar measure, with the Christian believer. It is a distinguishing mark of the commonwealth to which he belongs, that love is not only the foundation-principle in the righteousness for which the commonwealth exists, but also the uniting-power which binds the community together — that the inspiration of the common life and of the individual life are thus the same. The Christian believer, therefore, cannot grow in his true development along the line of the ideas of the Christian state, unless he comes into vital union with the brotherhood of believers. But the *cannot* is not so much one of necessity, as one of privilege. It is *the blessed possibility* of life in the Christian commonwealth — not *the requirement of a stern and hard law* — that, through the binding force of that love for one another which rests upon the common love of the Lord for all, the individual believer may know within himself the influence of the communion of saints and so of what is universal in the brotherhood. The citizen of the civil state, even when he dwells by himself in a foreign land, is not a single personality, confined within the limits of his own being. As truly as he carries with him the freedom to which he was born, so truly does he possess in his mind and soul the life of the community and the state in which he was born. Wherever he may be, his thought and character, and his very self, are in-woven with what is innermost in all to whom has been given the same inheritance; and only thus, and for this reason, is he a true citizen. How much more truly, may we say, is this the fact in the case of the citizen of the heavenly commonwealth, in whom love moves ever parallel with faith, and for whom the life of the state is the life of the individual multi-plied, and united in its manifold manifestations, through an ever outgoing and incoming love.

A third element in the privilege of citizenship, which one carries with him whithersoever he goes, is the consciousness of his relation to the state and its government. The member of a strong common-wealth has within himself abroad, as well as at home, a kind of personal consciousness of the strength which the state possesses. He is strong, because of its power. He is firm, because of its stability. He has a deeper sense of his own man-hood, by reason of his assurance that the freedom which it has bestowed upon him is made secure by its ability to defend itself and him against all enemies. What was the significance, in this regard, of the words, I am a Roman citizen, to the Apostle who was now writing to the church in Philippi, where a few years before he had boldly challenged the magistrates of the city by the assertion of this claim! He knew that the power and glory of Rome were in the citizenship, and he rejoiced, with a noble pride, that he was born to this privilege. The citizenship in heaven had a similar significance to his thought. The kingdom to which I belong, he said to himself, is a kingdom which cannot be moved. Its immovable character passes into myself, as I enter into its membership. The agitations and oppositions and conflicts of the world cannot disturb my confidence or my peace. The seizure of my person for imprisonment or the hindrance of my work cannot shake my faith. All things are moving forward according to the plan of Divine wisdom, and the kingdom pertains to God.

And so — even, as it would seem, with less incoming of questioning or fear— may the believer of this quieter age take to himself the same thoughts. The warfare of the spiritual enemies of to-day is less dangerous, than that of the forces and governments of the earthly states was then, and the doubts and denials which the Christian finds about him on every side are only different in their character now from what they have been in other generations. They are not more formidable than those which have been overcome by the powers of the heavenly commonwealth many times in the past history. The triumphs already witnessed, therefore, bear testimony for the issue of the present and coming struggles. I may not disquiet my soul because I am pressed into the midst of them, or because I see them fiercely moving on about me, or even breaking in upon the Church itself. The ages tell me their own story, and it is one which brings calmness and peace. The immovableness of the kingdom has ceased to be a thing of promise only, and has become a thing of experience.

The citizen of the heavenly commonwealth thus has the privilege of rest and confidence in his soul. His inheritance and home are not in a weak state, which has no strength to defend and secure him in all his rights and blessings, and no influence or authority extending beyond its own borders. He is a member of the eternal commonwealth, and of the city which hath the foundations, and he can abide among strangers while he must do so, or in a foreign land, with a sense of the power and greatness of that which is eternal. His privilege, therefore, takes hold upon the assured existence of the state, as well as upon the life-principle pertaining to it, and the life-powers which inspire his own life and that of the community — and all the elements of privilege combine to ennoble him in his citizenship, while he experiences its blessings.

But this last point in the matter of privilege — the assurance of the permanency and immovableness of the power of the commonwealth — is closely akin to the hope which belongs to the heavenly citizenship. The Apostle points us towards this hope as he moves on in his words, and shows us that the possession of it is a chief ground of his glorying and his joy. The particular thing upon which his mind centres, indeed, is that in which it finds its consummation. But there can be no doubt that in the final completeness, to his thought, there are gathered up, as it were, and presupposed all those blessings the realisation of which prepares the way for the end.

If the state is permanent in its life and victorious in its power, it will fulfil its promises to its citizens. They may be but in a partial experience, for the present, of that which pertains to them in their right as members of the state. They may have only somewhat of the inner life of the home-country, while they are sojourning in another land far away, and may know only half of the privilege which they might otherwise enjoy. But they can look forward. It will not be thus always. The state will gather its citizens to itself, and will put them in full possession of that which it has within its own boundaries. It will bear them forward in the experiences of its distinctive and peculiar life, until it has realised for them all that it has to bestow.

The thought of Paul, which he indicates here and to which he gives more full expression elsewhere, is that from the beginning of the Christian course the spirit of the man becomes possessed of a new life — the true soul-life — because of righteousness, but that the work is finished only in the future when, at the end and the coming of the Lord, the last enemy, death, shall be destroyed, and the perfected spirit shall have united with the perfected spiritual body, the instrument of its action and the home for its dwelling forever. The movement of the heavenly commonwealth will be steadily onward until that time. The principle that animates and governs the life of the state — righteousness, founded on faith and inspired by love—which was implanted in the citizen at his entrance into it, gives to him this life. The life develops ever afterwards—as it can and may, while he is absent from his own country; as it must and will, when he comes into it;—and by and by, when it is perfected in fitness for the highest blessings, the outward and the inward are brought together in a beautiful union, and the soul has its building from God, its house not made with hands, eternal in the heavens. This is the perfected soul's dwelling-place in the eternal city—the commonwealth of God.

Hope thus moves along the line of the ever continuing progress and is, as we may say, essentially and vitally connected with it. It is a part of the life-power of the commonwealth and its citizenship, and rests upon the basis of what is enduring in the commonwealth itself.

Such is the Apostle's conception; and how can it be otherwise? The citizen in his absence from home looks forward, as by a necessity, to the hour of his return to his own country and to the fulness of blessing of the time which shall follow that hour. The greater his confidence in the strength and stability of the state to which he belongs, the more sure and undoubting is his hope. If the power is there, the result will be secured. The life that is stirring within him, and is growing towards the completeness which can be realised only in the experiences and surroundings of this home-country, is itself the evidence that the hope will not be disappointed. The citizenship involves and proves

the hope — and the citizen of the heavenly commonwealth may well glory in it.

But the privilege of the citizenship, as the Apostle
speaks of it, points backward to the thought of
duty, as well as forward to the thought of hope.
The citizen of the heavenly state has a duty as
related to it, while he is dwelling in another country.
It is interesting to notice that the words which Paul
uses are in accordance here, as they are in other
points, with the suggestion of the figure of the text.
The sojourner in a stranger's land, who makes that
land his home for a season, does not owe it to his
native country to be careless of the life about him,
or to neglect or refuse to mingle in it. He is not
under obligation to dwell apart, and decline to be
a true man among men. Quite the opposite of this.
The call of the home-country, as well as of his
manhood, is to do faithfully whatever lies before
him in the pathway of right and truth and service
and love, and to grow in his fitness for the blessing
of the home-life through the fulfilment of duties in
the life abroad.

But the duty of his citizenship to his native land
is to be the first of all things — so penetrating his
life with its influence and summoning his powers
towards itself, that his work and heart shall turn
homeward in their final purpose and deep devotion.
And this is Paul's thought of the Christian believer.
He is to live *in the world*, but not to be *of it*. He
is to be earnest in the world's work as it falls to him
to do it, and to live as a man for the progress and

welfare of the world; but he is not to *mind earthly things;* — that is, the bent and direction of his mind — his desires, and purpose, and will, and soul itself — are not to be toward earth, but toward heaven. He is to keep in thought, always, that his citizenship is in the heavenly commonwealth, and that the fulness of his life towards which he should be ever moving is there. The duty of his years of sojourning and absence from home is to be in the line of the hope which pertains to his citizenship, and of the privileges also. We cannot separate the hopes and privileges of our citizenship from its duties. They combine together in the citizen's life. They are a part of himself, wherever he may be. As he glories in the privileges and rejoices in the hopes, so he must consecrate himself to the duties. Thus only can he be a citizen, in the true and full sense of the word.

The Christian life is a peaceful, happy one. It has the three elements of such a life — duty, and privilege, and hope. It moves on heavenward while it abides on earth, ever bearing within itself the knowledge of its origin and its future. It gathers into itself all good, and puts forth its powers for all helpfulness and service in the earthly sphere; but it grows, as by the impulse of its own nature, under the influences of the heavenly sphere. Its permanent and joyful peace will be there.

X

FOR MY SAKE

Jesus said, Verily, I say unto you, There is no man that hath left house, or brethren, or sisters, or mother, or father, or children, or lands, for my sake, and for the gospel's sake, but he shall receive a hundredfold now in this time, houses, and brethren, and sisters, and mothers, and children, and lands, with persecutions, and in the world to come eternal life.—MARK x. 29, 30.

THESE words, which are recorded after substantially the same manner in all of the first three Gospels, follow, according to each of the narratives, immediately upon the story of the conversation between Jesus and the rich young ruler. As the young man turned away sorrowful, when the demand was made that he should give up his possessions, and distribute to the poor, as the condition of entrance into the soul's true life, Jesus called the thoughts of the disciples to the great and almost insurmountable difficulty which those who loved riches had in forsaking them for the kingdom of God. In response to what He said, Peter, speaking for himself and his companions, reminded Him that they had left their homes and everything to become His followers, and then, in the line of the suggestion of the moment, asked the question as to what the reward should be for doing this. The answer to the question was given in this general form, and with application to all disciples. Let us consider some part of the teaching which the words suggest to us respecting the Christian's service and reward.

The expression which holds the central place in the order of the words and in the thought, is the expression " for my sake." These words are fundamental to the Christian doctrine everywhere. The disciple asks for, and receives forgiveness, at the outset of his new life, for the sake of Jesus. He consecrates himself to duty in His name. He makes the work to which he devotes his energies a work for Him. He offers his petitions to God for needed gifts, and presents his thanksgiving for past blessings only through Him. He finds the inspiration which moves him to manly living and to service for the good of men in his love for Him. He abides in the joy of his own thoughts, and grows in the sweetness and beauty of character in the hope of His approval. He looks forward to the future with the most delightful anticipation, because he is then to be with Him and to be like Him. From the beginning he lives for Him, and at the end he even dies for Him. The personal relation of the soul to Jesus is insisted upon, under all circumstances, as essential to that life of true righteousness which is acceptable to God; and in this personal relation is declared to exist the life-giving force which opens the way into it, and impels the soul forward in it.

So it is represented here. When the first act is

spoken of by which, in the light of the call to the
young ruler that had just been given, the entrance
into the kingdom is pictured forth — an act of self-
sacrifice and of leaving possessions, or home, or
family — it is described as done for the sake of Jesus.
It is not simply that self is sacrificed or duty is fulfilled, but chiefly, and above all, that the offering
and fulfilment are for Him. The answer of Jesus
was an answer to Peter's word, "We have left all
and followed thee." It was an answer which met
the demands of the case that was presented, and
which promised a reward to the action of those, who,
like him, had left their homes and their possessions
to the end of the following.

What, we may ask, are the elements of power in
this great motive and impulse of the Christian life,
as they are indicated in the two verses? The first
element is found in the leaving of all things for the
sake of a friend. It is sometimes claimed that this
is not the noblest ground of self-sacrifice — that
consecration to duty for its own sake, and because
it is right, is more worthy of the truest manhood,
than any devotion which rises out of personal affection. But no one can doubt that in such affection
there lies a powerful incentive, which must affect
and energise the soul. Friendship, wherever it
exists, bears witness to its force. It testifies, also,
that it is effective for the upbuilding of character.
Upon this force Christianity lays hold. The man
whom it approaches, and who has lost the true
righteousness, is pointed to a Friend who has loved

him. This Friend has seen his fall into sin, his
hopeless condition, his forfeiture of the blessedness
of union with God, his dark prospect for the future.
He has seen, also, how fatally sin has wrought by
its influence upon his soul, so that the eye of the
soul has been dimmed, or even blinded, to the
beauty of what is good, and its faculties have been
weakened in their outgoing towards right affection
or right action. Moved by the sight, He has drawn
near to help him. He has entered, as far as possible, into his limitations and temptations; into his
experiences and possibilities; into his weakness
and darkness; and has offered him all things for
the future — forgiveness, to meet and set aside his
sin; light, to illumine the darkness into which he
has fallen; strength coming from a Divine source,
to enable him to resist evil; a pure and perfect
example for him to imitate; a beautiful life to inspire and allure him by what it has to give; and a
hope reaching into the invisible, which carries in
itself the promise of a glorious realisation. The
Friend thus raises him from death to life — a death
the reality and sadness of which he apprehends
more fully, as the new life begins and moves forward in its course. He is, in a sense in which no
other friend is or can be, the author of all things
on which the man now centres his thought and his
hope. When the words "for my sake" are spoken
by such a friend, and accompany the request or
demand to leave houses, or lands, or anything that
seems good, what a living and life-transforming
power they must bear with them! Who that real-

ises what the things which have been done, and those which are offered, are, can fail to respond to these words with the answering sacrifice of all things at the very door of the new life?

The motive may not, indeed, affect every man, for it may not be that every man will believe in the story of what the Friend has accomplished in his behalf, or even that He is a friend. But where it finds entrance into the soul far enough to stir the vital forces, it must stir them as with a mighty energy, and in the direction in which the friend calls them forth. This impulse also, whatever we may say of the comparative measure of nobleness which belongs to it, cannot but be an added power for the soul's movement, beyond anything which can spring from the sense of right, or devotion to duty — the power of personal affection, of gratitude and love.

Why did Peter and his companions leave all and follow after Jesus, while the young man who had just departed, turned back to his great possessions sorrowful? Because they had received into themselves, as he had not, this power. From the first day of their meeting with the wonderful teacher, they had learned from His words and His actions how much He had done for them. They saw in Him at the beginning a light, which shone more and more brightly as the days passed, and they believed that He had brought a great blessing to their lives, and had wrought a great work in their behalf. The thought of Him grew richer and the love for Him grew deeper, and a wonderful force for the life came with the love and the thought.

When the call was made for the life-service and the life-fellowship, the soul at once responded to the influence. They forsook all which had filled their minds and moved their hopes before, and gave themselves to Him and His work. They rose up immediately as He summoned them, and went after Him in *His way*, not *their own*. This, also, was but the beginning. In the inner life, as well as the outer, they listened to His voice ever afterward. They heard in their deepest souls the words " for my sake," and they moved on to new duty, and new love, and new hope — realising within themselves the meaning and impulse of the divine fellowship. And thus it has always been, from that early time to ours. These tender and heart-moving words, which bear witness of so much in the life of the great Friend, and of the disciple, also, in his discipleship, have possessed for all believers the secret of the vital force which has made them ever ready after the same manner to follow Him.

The verses, however, suggest another element in the power of the motive. The words, " for my sake," are joined with the words, "for the gospel's sake." The forms of expression used by the different evangelists at this point are quite significant, as they are compared with each other. Matthew has the expression, " for my name's sake," Mark has, " for my sake and the gospel's," Luke has simply, " for the kingdom of God's sake." The sacrifice and service, which are demanded for the sake of the friend, are demanded for the kingdom. The whole matter is centred in the one thing, or the other, or in the two together, according as the thought is directed towards it from one place of observation or from another. It is in this way that the motive becomes the noblest one possible, for — while it bears in itself the force and inspiration of affection for a friend, who has given all things, and even himself, for those who needed his help — it also moves the man by the impulses which send him forth to unselfish service on behalf of the world. The person and the kingdom become in this sense one, and the love which goes out in gratitude towards the person for what he has accomplished for the individual soul, goes forth also, and by the very necessity of the case, in helpfulness for all others.

The Christian's love is not, therefore, and cannot be, other than benevolent and all-embracing. It cannot ever, while it remains itself, become, as the love of earthly friendship sometimes does, a thing in the enjoyment of which the possessor of it indulges for himself alone, and thus unworthy of his purest and most exalted manhood. But moving along the same line of grand unselfishness in which the spirit of consecration to right and duty moves, it unites the most exalted impulses belonging to the heart with those which rise from thought and moral principle, and thus urges the man forward, as by the common life-force of his whole being. It supplies for him, and in him, what the mere moral sense and the obligations of the soul to the law of righteousness can never of themselves furnish — and the thing which it gives is a wonderful power for the development of character, and for its outworking in all good service.

Jesus entered our human life, and fulfilled His work among men, and suffered and died, in order that the Gospel might be made known, and the kingdom established. He made all men His brethren to this end, and as He tenderly and graciously told the story of the love of God, He revealed impressively His own self-sacrifice in love to all. The significance of His work was to be found in the Gospel and the kingdom. When He summoned His followers, therefore, to leave possessions and friends for His sake, He called them, at the same time and by the same act, to give themselves to the kingdom. They were to devote their lives to the cause to which He had devoted His life. They were to tell the story, and labour for the kingdom, and bear witness of the true righteousness, and proclaim the way of faith, and make God known as ready to forgive and to save all who would turn to Him — placing this work above all others, with whatever of self-sacrifice it might involve. They were to do it for His sake, because they had for themselves, and their own souls, received such inestimable blessings from Him. But, as they did it for His sake, they were to give themselves, in the deep and true understanding of the meaning of these all-inspiring words, *for His sake*, — and in a love and service, after their measure, like His own, — to the extending of the same blessings to their fellow-men. To leave all things for my sake — such is His word to His disciples — is to leave all things for the Gospel's sake. To tell the

Gospel story, and thereby bring in the realisation of the kingdom, is to do the work of God's righteousness with an abounding and unselfish love. And so the motive power of the words, " for my sake," is a soul-stirring and all-victorious force.

The verses suggest, also, another element in the power of the motive, which we may well notice for a moment. By the call, which is given, to leave all things for His sake, Jesus puts Himself in comparison not only with houses and lands — that is, the great possessions, which had proved sufficient to keep the young ruler from entering the gateway of life, even when he saw it opening before him — but also with brethren, and parents, and children. The friendship of Jesus is set above he nearest and truest earthly friendships, and the suggestion is thus given of what it is for the soul. The impelling force of which we are speaking is found in the character of the Friend and of the personal relation with Him. The weakness or even selfishness of human love, as it exists at times between two friends, is connected closely with the imperfection which pertains to human character. The higher the one whom we love rises in the beauty and glory of manhood, however, — the more nearly he approaches the perfection which we picture to ourselves, but do not realise, — the less are we in danger of making the love minister to self, as we exercise and enjoy it. This must be so, because the influences that come through such a personal relation are those which move from the inmost life of the one party in

the union into the inmost life of the other. This
life in the centre and fountain of the soul being all
purity, and truth, and self-sacrifice, and readiness
for faithful service, the teaching and the impulse
which come from it must be of the same character.
The man of magnanimous feeling, or lofty purpose,
or elevated sentiment, or sweet reasonableness, or
warm affection, inspires his intimate and loving friend
with what goes forth from himself, and by means of
the inspiration brings him into his own likeness.
This inspiration is a transforming and purifying and
glorifying power which works with continual, though
oftentimes, it may be, with silent energy. It is,
moreover, a power which is recognised, as its results in the life are seen, with the deepest gratitude.
When the request for service or sacrifice, accordingly, presents itself from such a man to such a
friend in the words, " for my sake," there is hidden
in these words a secret force that reveals itself more
and more clearly — and with an ever-increasing
energy — as the call seems to sound along the
avenues of the soul, awakening there the remembrance of all the influence which has come from the
one to the other. It can only be a power for good
action, for the source from which it springs is the
goodness of another's character. It can only be a
power in harmony with true and generous feeling,
because the generous life of one soul must pro-
duce generous life in another. Its measure can
be estimated only by experience. The soul determines it for itself.

The life of Jesus, however, was the life of perfect

manhood, beyond any other that the world has known. This is the thought of all respecting Him, whatever differences there may be in the other thinking of men as to His nature or His work. What then must have been the influence which passed from Him to those who sat beside Him, and lived in His society and fellowship! They must have been conscious as the years passed on, that they were growing larger in their manhood, and nobler in their soul's living in every part of it, by reason of their nearness to His thought and love and perfectness. And when the call came, which they obeyed, to follow Him in anything, and anywhere, for His sake, they must have felt that the love of Jesus, which constrained them, was the most divine motive which could impel their souls.

The words " for my sake," therefore, as they read their true lesson to us and speak of their true meaning, tell us of an incentive for life which rejects from itself all that is unworthy, or of self alone, and which gathers into itself in different ways, and through varied thoughts, the most effective force for the transformation of character — a force which allies itself actively with every other that inspires for good, and gives new energy to every other.

It is a force also which works towards a reward. The verses of the evangelist tell us of this, and, as in the case of the motive-power, they reveal to us something of its nature. The Christian doctrine lays hold, for its followers, of the influence derived from hope. It promises a blessedness in the future,

in recompense for the sacrifice of the present. But
as it turns the mind of the one who believes it away
from selfishness, when it imparts to him its impulse
at the beginning, and along the course, so it does
the same thing when it points to the end. The
reward that it offers is one which belongs only to
the unselfish soul. The words of Jesus show this.
The very peculiarity of the call to leave all things
suggests the idea. The man who would be a disciple
is bidden to sacrifice himself. Possessions, it may
be great ones; friends, even the nearest and most
precious; a chosen and happy way of living, and a
work for one's own growth and to one's own advantage; these things, and things like them, must be
given up, if the true life is to be gained. The intimation of such a demand is, that the true life, and
whatever rewards there may be connected with it,
are to be found only in a sphere where self cannot
reign supreme. And the intimation is strengthened,
when the leaving of all is called for, not that one
may serve his own purpose or gain his own end, but
for the sake of a kingdom and a gospel which pertain to the true righteousness — the fruit of love
and of faith. It is made still further impressive,
when it is declared that all is to be done for the
sake of a friend whose whole work was an offering
of himself on behalf of others, and whose self-sacrificing love led him even to die for the world.

But — apart from and beyond these intimations —
the words themselves which describe the reward
give their own suggestion. The assurance and
promise are presented in the verses in two parts.

In the former part, which sets forth what is promised in this world, the description of the reward is given, after a manner which is characteristic of Mark's Gospel, in expressions answering to those employed in the giving of the call and demand. As the *sacrifice* is of houses and lands and friends, so the *recompense* is said to be in a greater measure of the same gifts. But the conversation with the rich ruler, and the sayings which follow after it with respect to the love of riches, as well as the very peculiarity of the expressions themselves, make it manifest that their meaning is not to be discovered in a literal interpretation of them, but in the thought which the occasion and the context place beneath and within the words. Interpreted thus, they teach us the truth to which all Christian experience bears witness, that for the self-sacrificing soul the possessions which are left behind, and which pertain to the outward life, are replaced, as it were, by possessions of the inward life. The joy of Christ, which came through His offering of Himself in obedience to the Father's will, is imparted to His followers. His peace becomes theirs. The hope and blessedness of the Gospel enter into their souls. They take hold upon all that is heavenly, rather than earthly, in character; and the life within them which is worthy of the name in all its full significance — the soul life — is saved.

This is, indeed, in accordance with the very law of self-sacrifice. The soldier, who consecrates himself to the service of his country and goes to the front in battle for its well-being, must leave his possessions behind him, but he gains a hundredfold in the loss of them. He knows *within himself* something which is far better, even as it is far grander, than that which he once had and which was *without himself.* The man who renders self-denying service in love for a friend knows the same experience, only in smaller measure, it may be, by reason of the more limited nature of the service rendered. This manifolding in the inward life is the rich experience which the years bring to all of us, if we are noble men. But the manifolding is to the limit of the hundredfold for the Christian disciple, because he gives himself to the greatest of all causes, that of God and man alike, and offers his service, in sacrifice of self, for the sake of a Friend who is above and beyond all others.

The continual movement towards him of love is also realised in his experience, as it comes from those who, by reason of his leaving all things for the Gospel and the kingdom's sake, are themselves brought to the membership of the kingdom and the full blessing of the Gospel. This love is ever repaying him, by its gifts, for the sacrifices which he has made.

In the early time, when the words of Jesus were first spoken, the new love, which had a purer and more sacred element in it than the old love had, was the whole, and indeed the sufficient, recompense for what was given up. But, in these later and Christian ages, the love of the old friends, who are left behind for the sake of Jesus and the kingdom, oftentimes becomes itself a holier affection for this very reason, and realises by its ever-increasing power a special reward for the self-sacrificing disciple. The gift thus bestowed — when viewed in relation to friendships or possessions — seems even to be a multiplication of those which were enjoyed before; and in the deeper satisfaction of the soul, and the richer blessing of its experience, the literal fulfilment of the words, as it were, comes to pass — now, in this time, a hundredfold in houses, and lands, and brethren, and friendships; now, in this time — so truly does the Gospel bear within itself the promise of the life that now is, as well as of that which is to come.

Indeed, its second promise only grows out of, and follows in the same line of blessing with, the first. The eternal life is only the fulness of that which enters the soul at the time of the leaving of all things for the Divine Friend's sake, and which abides there afterwards. It is no outward reward which can be selfishly sought after, like so many of the recompenses of the earthly career. It is the perfecting of holy character in love and every grace and beauty — the very beginning and ending of which is the loss of self in faithful service, and in the doing and living for His sake.

How impressively is this taught us by that single other word which Jesus adds to the picturing of the earthly rewards — *with persecutions*, a word which, through the victories of the faith, has lost for us its depth of meaning known so well by the first disciples, yet still has an abiding force in the tests and trials which beset us all. These, as the verses assure us, move on with the reward, and work into it continuously. The perfectness of the result at the end is reached, in part, by means of their mysterious working. But their working is ever, through losses and sacrifice of the outward, into the growth and development of the inward. The soul becomes wonderfully stronger through that which it loses. It *finds itself*, when it gives up all things. And thus its growth into its own fulness, through what were *in the old time* persecutions, and are *now* trials and sorrows, is ever realising for it more perfectly the banishing of selfishness in the discovery of its true self. The movement is a beautiful and a grand one, in the line of the manliest living, from the first act of sacrifice for His sake to the final experience of reward in the eternal future. What a blessed assurance it is, which the words give to us all, if we will listen to them : There is no man who has left all for me and for the Gospel, but he will receive a hundredfold in his soul's experience here, and the eternal life of the soul hereafter.

XI

THE TRUE SEER

And one of the Pharisees desired him, that he would eat with him. And he entered into the Pharisee's house, and sat down to meat. — LUKE vii. 36–50.

[The verses contain the story of the woman who anointed the feet of Jesus in the Pharisee's house.]

I WOULD offer for consideration a few thoughts which are suggested by this story as we look at it from certain special points of view. In the first place, it has a revelation for us as to the method by which Jesus met the difficulties of those who questioned His claims as a teacher of the Divine truth, and, though not meeting Him with hatred or with obstinate rejection of His words, were yet unwilling to come to Him for the truth until these difficulties should be removed. The person whom the story represents as inviting Jesus to his house was one of the Pharisees. We are told nothing else with definiteness concerning him. But we may infer, from the indications of the verses, that his purpose in giving the invitation was not a hostile one, such as we find manifested by others of the sect to which he belonged as they came into contact with Jesus. He did not desire, apparently, to catch Him in His talk, as the sacred writers express it, or so to entangle

Him in His answers to what he asked, that he might have some foundation for accusing Him before the authorities of the nation. He simply wished to satisfy himself, as we may believe, as to whether Jesus was worth listening to and whether He had any message from Heaven. He thought that by offering Him his hospitality he would have Him alone by Himself, and thus could, in the best and most successful way, determine the matter which he had in mind. Everything in the story points to this as the correct supposition respecting him. Its consistency with the details which are mentioned, and the explanation which it presents for the absence of certain details which we might otherwise have expected to find, render it so probable that we may without hesitation accept it. This Pharisee, therefore, was a questioner in the sphere of righteousness and life, as all members of his party were in greater or less degree, so far as they were truly worthy of a place within it. He would know what Jesus had to say, and would test Him.

If this is the right view of the matter, we may believe that, for the carrying out of his purpose, he had his direct questions in mind — many of them, perchance — which he was prepared to present. He was ready to offer them so soon as the supper should have proceeded far enough to make it fitting to do so. He was waiting, perhaps impatiently, for the proper moment to come. But suddenly, and by an accident as it seemed, a new turn was given to his thought, and a question which appeared to him fundamental to all others was started in his mind.

It was a question of doubt as to whether Jesus was a prophet-teacher at all — whether He had any prophetic relation to the truth whatever.

According to a custom of the region and of the time, which allowed strangers to enter unbidden at such a meal, and to approach the guests and speak with them, a woman suddenly came into the room where they were, and at once drew near to Jesus and proceeded to anoint His feet with ointment which she had brought. This person was, as the writer tells us, a sinner. Evidently she was, to the mind of the Pharisee, a sinner of so marked a character that her very touch was a defilement. The current of his thoughts was immediately arrested. The difficulties connected with his old system of belief rushed in upon him at once, and the inquiries after the truth must, as he felt, wait until these were settled. Is the man a prophet at all? he said to himself. A prophet, surely, would know what sort of a person this is. But apparently he does not know. A prophet must not suffer himself to be defiled. But he is allowing this to happen, with no resistance or objection. The manifest presence of the sinner here, does it not prove that there is no prophet here? My questions, which I had promised myself the asking, are useless until this matter is determined ; and I do not see how it can be determined except unfavourably for the professed teacher. So long as this difficulty, thus suggested, remains, he can have nothing for me. The teacher, surely, must precede the teachings, and be the authority for them. I doubt his right to the teacher's office, and I do not believe that he can establish it. What I had hoped for fails, and I may well allow him to depart.

We may observe with interest how Jesus met his difficulty. He did not meet it by argument, or by a renewed and emphatic assertion of what He claimed for Himself. He did not attempt to show him directly or by reasoning that his view of the matter of pollution was a narrow one, founded upon a mere superficial view of the letter of his own system. He did not enter at all into the sphere of his questionings. He went behind all this, and farther down into the depths of human experience. He said to him in briefest words: Let me tell you a simple story of common life. A money lender had two debtors, to one of whom he had lent ten times as much as he had to the other. Time passed on. The debts became due, and when he found that both alike had nothing wherewith to pay him, he forgave them both. The story is a very simple one — is it not? It has not much to do with the question whether a man has a prophetic gift from God, or is a divinely-commissioned teacher, you may think. Be it so, if you will — at least, for the moment. We will wait for the decision of that question, which will come in its own time. But its own time is not now. Now is the time for something other than this. How will it be about what follows the forgiveness? Which of the two men, who have their debts forgiven, will love the kindly friend the most? There cannot be much doubt as to this point, surely. We may dispute about the other question, but we shall agree in our answer to this: The one to whom he forgave the most. Let us make our starting-point then where we agree, and after this look outward in two directions. There are two matters on which your mind is resting — righteousness, and my claim to be a prophet. The one is a matter of the soul's life; — the other, as you put it, a question of the mind's thinking. You are placing the latter before the former. You should place the former before the latter. If you move from the right beginning, you may hope to reach the right end. What then does the story tell you about the true righteousness? Think of this. It tells you how it originates, and what it is. Apply the story to real life, and you will understand it.

Thus he speaks with his questioner. The man who in his own view had lived in accordance with rules and had had few failures; who had made the letter of the law his study and had been punctilious in his observance of it; who regarded himself even as within the kingdom of God because of his birth and education, and had little sense of sin, makes no demonstration of love, because he has none. He is cold and formal and critical, because there has been no deep movement of his soul and no sense of ruin or danger. The sinner, on the other hand, who is conscious of the fact, and who therefore feels his need of help and of deliverance, is the one who is on the way to the true life, because the soul within him is stirred. He knows where he stands, and will love the Divine helper who lays hold upon and helps him. It is when the soul is stirred that the life begins. All life shows this. What a new light the words were fitted to bring into the Pharisee's mind. The action of the woman, which seemed to his dull apprehension — dulled by his own self-righteousness and legalism and literalism — to be polluting in its character because she was a sinner, was in reality the evidence and outflow of that love which had within itself the power to overcome the sin and reform the life. Righteousness is not mere action. It is not mere conformity to the words of a law. It is such action and conformity founded upon a life-principle. Common life everywhere tells us this. Human experience, in its inmost and central sources, proves it. Look within yourself, and you will be a witness to the truth. Let the questions of life thus move within the sphere of life; — and when these questions are answered, it will be the time for further questioning.

And now, who is the prophet? The man who knows this, or the man who does not? The man who penetrates by his clear vision into the secret beginnings of human action as they are found in the first impulses of the soul, or he who never gets far enough below the surface of things to think of anything except the external defilement of meeting with one who has been a sinner? The prophet is a seer. Which of the two is it that sees? The prophet is inspired to understand the Divine idea of righteousness. Which of the two gives evidence of the inspiration? — The story of experience answers both of the questions, if they are placed in their right order. And why should it not — for the forces which are illustrated in human experience are the forces which move life, and the movement of life is that which makes the man. To know this is to see the truth, for all that is good centres in this movement.

Another revelation which the story has for us is, as to the way in which Jesus met those who came to Him from the starting-point of the deep wants of the inner life, and not from that of difficulties or intellectual questionings. The sinner in the story knew little, as we may believe — certainly, she thought little now — of the points in the legal system, which were filling, all at once, the mind of the Pharisee. Life had passed, to her apprehension, so far beyond the questions of external and ceremonial defilement, that this had become one of the minor and secondary things. The helper whose aid she felt to be necessary for her was one who should see the life's sources, and should purify and vitalise them. The sense of sin removed all difficulties but one from the mind. That one was, how to become free from sin's power. Everything in the narrative, moreover, seems to indicate that, even with regard to the great question of the renewal of character, she had but limited knowledge. She did not recognise her own faith, apparently. To the Pharisee's mind, she did not know enough to know her right position before a religious teacher, or to ask for forgiveness. Perhaps she had not thought far enough, to think of asking for it. But, in some way, the mind of this sinner had been turned to Jesus. From what she had seen of Him or heard of Him she felt that there was a great outflow of love and blessing in His soul, which was ready for all who would receive it. Possibly, she was conscious of having experienced already somewhat of its life-giving power. The confidence that the blessing was in Him, or the consciousness that the beginning of its influence had come to herself, led her to draw near to Him now, and to bestow upon Him a gift of affection and reverence. Her thought was wholly occupied with this one thing. If the Pharisee, or if Jesus Himself had asked her how she expected to secure the Divine forgiveness and to be set right with God, — what were the steps by which she would seek the gift, in order surely to attain it, or what was the precise pathway back from sin to righteousness, — she would probably have found herself unable to answer. She would certainly have said that all this was aside from her thought at the moment. She was now thinking only of an act of love, — perchance, of grateful love, — and in this was the whole purpose of her entering the house where they were. How different was her condition from that of the Pharisee! The difference was that which always exists — which manifests itself a thousand times to every careful observer of human nature, and is illustrated by examples everywhere—between the cold and doubting questioner who stands outside of the Christian system, and sees difficulties on every side for the mind to grapple with, and the man who knows that sin is a deadly evil, and feels its power within himself to be too great for his own strength to overcome.

But what did Jesus say to the sinner? He did not ask questions concerning her feeling; or try to draw from her a story of the way in which her mind was now turning; or bid her place her present thoughts and impulses beside the true order of the plan of forgiveness and the new life, and thus set her upon an examination of herself; or even in any way attempt to make her look into the movement of her soul, in order to determine its character or its reality. With the seer's eye which belongs to the true prophet, He saw for Himself, in the act which she had just performed, all that He needed to see, and then, with the same seer's eye, He saw that she was not yet prepared to study the movement.

But He turned to the Pharisee, and said, Seest thou this woman? Let the story of the debtors apply itself to you and to her, and study the question of the forces of life, as you make the application. You will find what you do not yet know — what she herself does not yet fully realise — that these forces are behind the act, and thus that the true life has begun in her, while you are still questioning and doubting. Then He details what she had done, in contrast with what the Pharisee himself had done, and shows by the repetition and the contrast the reality of the vital force — that her action was the overflowing and outpouring of a love which involved all things in itself. The very essence of the living righteousness, which had been lost out of the Pharisee's conception of it, was in this love. The love, therefore, may prove, even to your questioning mind, he says to him at the end, that the sinner whose presence here so troubles you,— however many her sins have been, and they have indeed been many,— has come into a new position. Her sins are forgiven, and the Divine renewal has begun. She has found God's righteousness, while you have lost your way utterly in seeking your own.

Moreover, He does not even tell what she has done, or picture the beauty of her act by its contrast, to the sinner herself. He lets her hear it, but does not set it before her as an explanation of the way in which she had come to be forgiven. So far is He from dealing with her after the manner of an examiner into the evidences of character, or according to the successive stages of a plan, — He says nothing at all of the relation of her love to her forgiveness, except to the Pharisee, and to him nothing except that he might know that she was forgiven, by reason of the evidence of the new life-power which her love gave. Indeed He says nothing in any way to herself, until all this had passed. The reasoning, the explanation, the pointing to the forces of life, were needed only for the questioning Pharisee. His dull mind—dulled by his own doubting — must have some answer. For the sinner, who was as yet moving according to the simplest of the nobler impulses of the soul, and was not ready to ask or understand the explanation, or to know anything of the philosophy of life, there was nothing until the end, and then only the one word of assurance.

Surely there is a lesson which is full of suggestion for us in the story, as we read it thus. But there is

another revelation which it has for us, as we notice
what He said to the sinner, after those who were
at the table with Him had expressed their astonishment at His assuming the power of forgiving sin.
He now tells the woman herself the great truth of
her renewed life — how it originated: Thy faith
hath saved thee. The woman did not apprehend
the truth at the time. Those who sat at meat with
Jesus did not apprehend it. The questioning Pharisee, no doubt, had his mind closed against it as the
words were uttered, for his thought and view of
righteousness had been altogether in another line.
But the words, nevertheless, contained the central
point of the Christian teaching, and they declare the
truth for all. The faith was saving because it was
an active force. It went forth in a heartfelt confidence towards the source of help. It laid hold,
believing, upon the blessing which was offered, and
upon the one who offered it. And as it went forth,
it proved itself to be a uniting power between the
souls, which opened the way for all life-giving influence to pass from the greater Friend to the
weaker one, and all loving feeling and action to go
from the one who needed help to the one who gave
it. The life-time afterwards was but the unfolding
of what was here said. Faith originated what love
proved. Faith worked, through the love-element in
it, towards all good; and love grew deeper and
richer, as faith became more and more beautifully
an undoubting confidence.

We question the Christian system from outside of
it, and then from inside of it; and we involve our-

selves, how often, in difficulties everywhere. What
is the relation of faith to love, we ask from the outer
position, and the inner one also; and, Has the
movement of the two been, in our individual experience, we say to ourselves, just what it ought to
have been? We can separate the two things in our
philosophy, and in our setting forth of the plan.
But *in human life* they move, many times, in such
close and intricate intermingling, that they can
scarcely be recognised in their independence. The
man distresses himself in seeking after faith, when
the *loving* actions of his life bear clearest testimony
to its existence. Or he deceives himself, perchance,
by the thought that his love has no divine origin or
evidencing power, when, if he will look into his
soul's workings, he will see that everything in the
inward, or the outward, life is inspired by an undoubting confidence and trust in the Divine Friend.
The faith, as in every union of souls, is the first life-
producing force. The love is the offspring and the
proof—the flower and fruitage — of the faith. But
they abide together through the years, working
harmoniously in every line, and become so nearly
one that the man only knows the oneness —the
believing love and the loving belief. Yet the faith,
notwithstanding this, ever saves, and the love
proves; and the answer of both together to the
man's questionings as to himself is: Thy sins are
forgiven.

There is one more revelation or suggestion which
the story gives, as it leaves us. The last word

addressed to the sinner bids her go in peace.
There is no such last word to the Pharisee. So far
as we are told, he remains in the midst of his questionings and his difficulties — waiting for the answering and removing of them by some explanation
which shall be more direct, and shall be more satis-
factory to his mind or his reasoning powers. The
accident of the hour had brought him very near to
the gate of the true life. But he could not suffer
Jesus to open it for him, because an old thought
connected with his old system of opinions made him
doubt whether Jesus was, after all, a prophet. How
could a prophet stand by the gate with such a sinner and allow himself to be defiled by a polluting
touch. Settle the difficulty first, and look for the
life afterwards. So it is always with the doubting
questioner — in this age, as in the first age — in our
company, as in the company of those who were at
the table with Jesus on that memorable day. The
error into which the doubter falls is a fundamental
one. Christianity deals with life. It is life. Its
working moves along the line of the soul's deepest
and truest experience. It is the most natural of all
things, as it moves thus. What could be simpler or
truer than the movement of the renewing forces in
the case of this sinner, of whom the story tells us?
Who can question for a moment the reality of the
power which was within her as she came to Jesus,
and as she went forth from His presence? And
who that understands anything about human experience, and the relations of one soul to another,
can fail to see, that peace and forgiveness are

vitally related to faith and love as she manifested them?

Christianity goes with us, indeed, into the mysteries of life and of thought. It answers many questions and unfolds many mysteries for us as we move patiently, and with open and honest minds, through the years. But its office is not to remove difficulties, but to remove sin. Its mission and purpose are not to satisfy the mind in all its inquiries and reasonings, but to give new life to the soul. The mind may fall into disbelief anywhere in the sphere of life and its impelling forces. It may originate it for itself and by its own efforts. You can doubt friendship, or family love, or patriotism, or true righteousness — and can lose them all in your doubtings — if you put yourself outside of them, as it were, and refuse to believe until every difficulty which your philosophy or your scepticism may start is set aside. They are, however, none the less real on this account. Their very life and sweetness and power belong in another sphere than that of the difficulties, and the questioning of the soul which brings it to the door of the sphere where they belong is the only one which reaches the blessing.

So is it with Christian living. What an insignificant thing as related to this, was the question whether Jesus was a prophet who had never been defiled by the touch of a sinner, and thus a prophet who could meet the demands of the Pharisee's preconceived ideas. What a momentous one, on the other hand, it was, that He was a seer into life — a man who knew the way to forgiveness, and right character — that character which comes out of the purified fountains of the soul, and is, when it thus comes, the grandest and most real thing in existence. Life has its own laws and its own forces. The way to live is the way of discovering the forces and using them. Doubts and questionings are not life. They are, rather, its opposite. Life is positive. Life is movement. Life is faith in the reality of things. Life is love which animates and inspires and glorifies the soul. The sinner of the story — many as her sins had been — had life, at this hour. The Pharisee had doubtings, and no noble impulse which stirred the man.

And so peace came to the one, but not to the other. The peace of the soul is the result of faith. The man who doubts and questions cannot be at rest. The settlement of his questionings must be secured before quietness and truest happiness can be his. But when faith enters the heart as an active power, and puts forth its energy through love, and unites the soul with God, — then the Divine gift comes in answer to the faith. The man lives, and works, and moves in all his movements after the Divine manner. There is peace in believing — an ever-abiding, ever-deepening peace. Jesus knew this, and knew the way to realise it. He was a seer who saw the centre of the soul and saw how it could be purified. He was one whom no sinner with the true life-impulse within him could defile by his touch, for He carried within Himself the transforming power through which all life is made holy. He was the helper for the sin-burdened man, and the one who spoke, as with the Divine voice, the word of forgiveness for the past and peace for the future. If you will place yourself near to Him, my friend, as He stands at the gateway of life, you will find the great blessing. As you recognise in Him the seer who sees the sources and forces of the soul's living, you will also discover Him to be the true prophet of the truth and of the ages.

XII

Let him that stole steal no more. — EPHESIANS iv. 28.

THE words of this sentence are a part of the practical section of the epistle addressed by Paul to the Ephesian Christians. They form one of the elements which make up the leading exhortation of the letter: that the readers should walk worthily of the calling wherewith they were called; and this exhortation, by the very manner in which it is introduced — I *therefore* beseech you — is founded upon the doctrinal teaching of the preceding chapters. They afford us, accordingly, an illustration of the way in which the Divinely-commissioned Apostle would bring the Christian truth to bear upon conduct. Examples, however, always pass in their teaching beyond their own immediate and narrow limits, and impress upon the mind not only particular lessons, but general ones. Let me offer some thoughts in connection with the words as bearing upon the results of our faith in our action and daily living.

In the first place, we may notice the immediate connection between this exhortation and the urgent request or demand, which the writer makes, that these Christians should hold firmly the true Chris-

166

tian doctrine. There is one Lord, one faith, one baptism, he says. In walking worthily of your calling, therefore, you should give all diligence to keep the unity of the Spirit and the unity of the faith. You should be careful not to be carried about with every wind, or to be tossed to and fro, after the wiles of error, but should possess, and cherish, and grow up more and more into the truth. But, in order to do this, and in doing it, you should cease — *because of the new life-principle in the inner life* — to give yourselves up any longer to the old practices of your former unchristian state, and should do what is right and good. The truth of the doctrine is to be sought for and to be maintained, for it alone is the Divine truth. But the doctrine has no vitality, and no fulness of meaning, without the true living which is the legitimate outgrowth of it. Hence the true living is the end, — the doctrine is only the means.

The Apostolic preachers were not the founders of a philosophical system, or professors in a school of theological science, to whose minds the setting forth of truth in definite and accurate and systematic formulas was the aim of their efforts or the object of their career. They were proclaimers of a way of salvation — of reforming and sanctifying the soul — of delivering mankind, and each individual man, from sin, and bringing all to righteousness. Their unfolding of the system which they taught was wholly for a practical end. We find them accordingly, in all their writings, placing the practical application to the personal and inmost life

after the doctrinal teaching and argument, and
making the latter preparatory to the former. They
did not enter into religious controversy for its own
sake. They did not stand on the watch-towers of
Zion to defend the truth simply as truth, but rather
to defend, and explain, and enforce it because they
believed it to be the only foundation of right living.
It was for the reason that the Christian teaching
would, through the working of its power within his
soul, lead the man who had been wont to steal to
do so no more — and for this reason as the first and
great and all-important reason — that Paul urged
upon him to guard himself against the deceits of
error, and to keep the faith. If the man succeeded
in holding the faith-system in its every minutest
point, so that the sleight of men or their cunning
craftiness could not move him in the smallest degree
from the form of sound words — so long as he did
not cease to steal his right belief was worthless, —
the Apostolic message had done him no good.

The claim which Christianity made for itself, as
it entered the world; the ground on which it asked
men to receive it, was, not that it contained a
system of doctrine beautiful to contemplate, but
that it presented the best, and even the only way of
developing the life of God in the soul of man. On
the satisfying of this claim its success in the world
must depend. The Master accepted the necessity
of the position which He assumed. By their fruits
ye shall know them, He set forth as the principle
of judging; and His immediate followers fully
recognised what He had set before them. As the

ages have moved forward, however, the Church has, many times, forgotten, or in large measure lost sight of this fact. It has, how often, given itself to fiery, and even savage discussion about the details of believing, and become careless and negligent about the heart-power of faith in the individual man, and its results in action. It has demanded the acceptance of doctrine as the essential condition of entrance into the heavenly kingdom, and has ceased to remember the Pauline word: If I know all mysteries and all knowledge in the Christian system, and if I have all faith so as to remove mountains, but have not love, I am nothing. But this is because the Church has not reached the standard of the Christianity which it professes, or been guided by the teaching of Christ and His Apostles in the truest and deepest meaning of it.

I ask you then, in the second place, to observe how Christianity approaches those to whom it offers its teaching. To take what will seem to us all, doubtless, one of the more extreme cases — how does it come to the man who has been a thief? It lays before him its doctrine of salvation by faith, in the simplest way, and asks him to accept it and make it a power — *the power* — in his life. How shall I do this? he says. The first thing for you to do, it answers — the special thing for you as an individual man — in developing the new life within you and opening the way for its fruitage is, to give up your old habit. Let him that stole steal no more. This ceasing to steal is, for you, the turning-point of your career. In this way only can you reverse your course, and free yourself from your sin. You may believe anything or everything — you may admire the precepts or doctrines given you by the New Testament — you may cultivate many virtues and have many good emotions, but if you continue your course of stealing, without effort to alter it, you are no Christian. After the same manner, as he goes on in his life — when the temptation and the weakness which come down to him from his old way of living make him liable to fall into sin, the same voice addresses itself to his mind and heart. Steal no more : — let this be the motto and maxim of your life.

Christianity does not say to such a man, guard yourself against drunkenness; perhaps the man has never been intoxicated in his life-time ; — nor, take care not to be angry; perhaps he is good-natured under all circumstances; — nor, let no corrupt speech proceed out of your mouth; possibly his speech is not corrupt. It does not divide its forces, or begin its attack upon him in the wrong place. It concentrates its energy upon that which is the centre of the evil, — that which stands in the way of the Divine life in the soul — and says, in a trumpet-tone and with a never-ceasing repetition, You have been a thief. Be an honest man.

The extreme character of the case supposed takes it out of our experience, but may only render its lesson more clear and more emphatic. It is a rare thing, no doubt, that one of our ordinary churches contains in its membership a man who lived, before his conversion, the life of a thief. The churches of the Apostolic age, whose members had been brought out of the vices of heathenism, may have had in their circle many such persons. But the message of Christianity is a similar one to all. As it opens its teaching to every man, it bids him cease to practise his own peculiar sins and become a new man. What is the membership of our churches? Not composed, indeed, of men who, in the vulgar sense, have been in the habit of stealing. But, in how many cases, of men who are willing to take advantage of their neighbours, or who in a petty way and in minor things fall below the highest standard of honesty, or who cherish their money as if it were the greatest good, or who are ungenerous, or are tyrannical in their families, provoking their children to wrath, or are so immovably obstinate as to make all who are dependent on them lose much of the happiness of life, or are so narrow-minded that they have no charity for others' views. To each of these classes of persons, and the many others of which we see examples in the churches of every name, the Christian teaching directs its demands just where they are needed. To the man who never gives away his money, for example, it does not say, first of all, Attend the weekly prayer-meeting; Give an hour daily to religious meditation; Establish family prayers in your house. Much less does it exhort him to give up slandering his neighbours — a thing which he has never had any impulse to do; or to avoid quickness of angry passion — to which his natural disposition is a stranger. It penetrates the inmost heart of his living, and bids him begin, and begin at once, to give away his money as he ought to give it. The love of that money is the stronghold of evil within his soul; and, until it is taken away in its all-controlling force, the work of Christianity is either not begun, or not perfected, in his case, no matter how sweet-tempered he may be, or how many hours he may spend in meditation. So to the obstinate man, it says, Lay aside your obstinacy; to the narrow-minded, Give up your narrow-minded-ness; to the man who is indolent, Be earnest and laborious; to each and every man, Cease to do the particular evil thing or things which you, personally and individually, are in the habit of doing. Build up character by beginning at the foundation.

It deals with men as John the Baptist did with the different classes who came before him. To the publicans, — as they asked him, What must we do? — he answered, Extort no more than that which is appointed you. This was the gateway of a righteous life in their case. To the soldiers, pre-senting the same question, his reply was, Do violence to no man, and, Be content with your wages. To the multitudes of selfish listeners, who desired to know his demand upon them, he said, He that hath two coats, let him impart to him that hath none, and he that hath food, let him do likewise. How simple the answer was. Be content with your wages. Be satisfied with your just dues. Be charitable and generous. The answer is the same to-day: Do the duty which lies directly before you in your individ-ual pathway. Abandon the wrong in your feelings, your action, your attitude towards others, your daily living, whatever it may be. Let the inward life-power which you receive from the new faith impel you to do thus. This is the way in which you are to begin or to go forward in the Christian course.

Whether you are a Christian believer already or not, my friend, the Christian teaching calls you to one thing: to look at your own life — not at mankind in general, or at the men around you, but at your own life — and to see what is your own evil habit or sin. Is it dishonesty, or unfaithfulness in the discharge of duties, or idleness, or censoriousness, or frivolity, or disregard of others' feelings, or any major or minor fault, as the world measures the greater and the less. Whatever it may be, — and we all know what it is, in the depths of our souls — the word that comes to us is: Put an end to it; overcome it; let its place be taken by the opposite virtue; just as to him that stole it is, Steal no more, but labour, working with your own hands, that you may have whereof to give to him that hath need. It is a thoroughly individual matter — this Christian doctrine. For this reason, it strikes at the root of character, and is truly reformatory of the life. It does not leave the inquirer or the disciple to fill his hours with mere meditation on the beauty of holiness, or even on the love of Christ — much less with passing judgment on sins of which some men, but not himself, are guilty. But it summons him, for the love of Christ and for His sake, to commit his own sins no more; and if it cannot persuade him to do this, its work for him is a failure.

We see thus, in the third place, that the success of Christianity in the world can be hoped for mainly — if not, indeed, only — from its success in this way in individual lives. We are passing, at present, through a season of great and widespread doubt. Everything connected with the Christian system is questioned or denied. The enemies of the faith are growing bolder, and its friends are sometimes prone to be discouraged. What — above all things else — is to check the evil, and to prove to mankind — to the doubters and deniers, even — the truth of our faith? The thing which can surely accomplish the end is, that every Christian believer should do just what has been referred to — put aside, by reason of his faith and because of its power within him, the wrong that is in his own life, and bring into its place the right. When this is done, the fruits will bear their own irresistible witness to the tree. The world will believe the doctrine, when it sees the life.

Let us take the case of a single community — the one, for example, in which we have our abiding place. Who can doubt that, if every professing Christian in such a community were to show to all about him that the Christian principle, implanted in his heart, was really overcoming the evils of his character, the power of Christianity would be multiplied tenfold throughout the community. And if it were so everywhere, how long would doubts about the truth of the system continue? We do not need laborious defences of the faith by able disputants so much as conformity to what the faith teaches in the daily actions which spring from the inner life of the man. Keep the unity of the faith, not by discussion and reasoning among yourselves or with the enemy, but rather by living and acting as true disciples of Christ. The power of the truth and the triumph of the faith are in the hands of each believer. He must be faithful to the charge committed to him, faithful in his own sphere and in his own life, or the victory will become so much harder to attain or so much longer delayed. If Christian men everywhere, and always, will practise the virtues — the common, human virtues, as they are sometimes called — which Christianity teaches, and will show by their lives that they practise them under the influence and teaching of Christian love, the sceptics will lose the power of their scepticism, so far as other men are concerned, and they will be the object of fear and apprehension no more.

Our train of thought thus far readily suggests to us, as a fourth matter of reflection, the answer to the question of duty for each and every Christian as he stands related to the church and to the world. Those who have recently entered the Christian life, and especially those who are young men or women, are often anxious about the matter of work. What shall they do as disciples of Christ? This matter of religious work has been made peculiarly prominent of late years, and many are perplexed about it — ready to put forth their efforts, but not knowing how, or when, or where. To such persons, and to all, the Christian teaching says: The great power of the truth in the world is the individual life — the inner life of the individual as manifesting itself by the outgoing of its own forces into true and righteous personal living among men. Your greatest power, my friend, lies in your ceasing, evidently to all around you, to be what you were as an unconverted man, and in being the opposite. What did Paul say to the Ephesian church members, old and young alike? He said, Let all bitterness, and wrath, and anger, and clamour, and railing be put away from you, with all malice. Let there be no covetousness, or uncleanness, or falsehood, or unfruitful works of darkness among you. Speak the truth, each one of you, with his neighbour. Let not the sun go down upon your wrath. If any one has been accustomed, in his former life, to steal, let him steal no more. In any and every way, be no longer a partaker with the sons of disobedience. Put off the old man from yourself, and put on the new man. Give to him that hath need. Be kind, tender-hearted, forgiving each other. If you are a child, obey your parents, and honour them. If you are a father, see that you do not provoke your children. Whatever your condition, walk in that condition worthily of the calling wherewith you were called. Be thus imitators of God, as dear children. This was the work which he gave these early Christians to do; and as they did it they commended the faith which they professed to all about them, and the Church grew in numbers and in power.

The same message comes to Christians everywhere, in our day. You desire, my friend, to do something for Christ — to exert an influence for

Him, and His cause, in the place and among the community where you live; and you ask, What is the work, and where is the opening for it? The Apostle's answer is: It opens in your own individual daily living. Your life may be very limited in its circle of action; it may be very wide in its range. But the message is the same. Are you a father? — I take an example from the life of those who are mature or older men — see how you are living with and before your household and your children. If you have been wilful, or tyrannical, or unsympathetic, or prone to insist upon your own views or wishes, to the disregard of those who are under your care — if you have not been tender-hearted or forgiving, considerate or magnanimous, free from wrath or bitterness — go home to your house to-day, and apply to yourselves the bidding which Paul gave to the men who had been stealing: that they should do so no more, but should live as honest and true men. Begin to be kind; put away wilfulness; let your children know that you are ready to consider their feelings, and not only their feelings, but their thoughts and opinions; show them that your own opinions are not held, and violently enforced upon them, because you inherited them from your fathers, or formed them under the influences of a former generation, which influences no longer exist. Be a Christian man, in all sympathy, gentleness, large-mindedness, self-sacrifice, sincerity, perfect truth — doing every duty of your position as a father, as Christ would have you do it.

How long a time would pass, my friend, before

your household would begin to feel the power of Christianity as they, perchance, had never felt it before? How long, before the knowledge and influence of your Christian living would reach men outside of your household, and they would begin to say to one another, and to themselves, There is a truth in the doctrine which that man professes to hold, for it has gone down into the recesses and fountains of his moral being, and made him a new and lovely man? And what Christian work for the neighbourhood, or town, or city, could be better than this? What work of yours could, by any means, be half as effective? But this lies directly before you, and may be begun in your own dwelling to-day.

You are a young man, perchance, just working your way into life. What is the call to you? To exhibit faithfulness in all little things; to be truthful, honest, upright; to be manly, earnest, devoted to what is good; to be kindly, ready for every service of friendliness, a generous Christian youth. There is work enough to do, without turning aside from that which God opens before you where you are. You need not seek it. It is present with you, and meets you at every step. Christ desires you to be a Christian in your own sphere, and in your own heart. By being so, you exert an influence greater than you can in any other way.

That positive Christian efforts for the religious welfare of the community — teaching, and exhortation, and persuasion, and benevolent aiding and giving, and the many other things which we think of as

connected with this matter — are demanded, no
Christian will deny. These things are of vast importance. They are a vital and essential part of the
duty of the Church. They constitute, in no incon-
siderable measure, that for which the Church exists.
But as we read the Apostolic letters to the early
churches — though the command to make known
the good-tidings everywhere is most clearly set
forth — it is a most noticeable and impressive fact,
that the burden of the practical exhortations, which
are represented as growing out of the Christian
truth, is not the fulfilling of this command, but the
developing of personal Christian life. How strikingly all the Epistles abound in urgent appeals to
the readers to be honest, honourable, merciful, pure,
generous, truth-telling, gentle; — not to be extor-
tionate, covetous, lovers of money, wrathful; — not
to be contentious, or given to much wine, or men-
pleasers, or full of envyings and jealousy; — not
to lie, or deceive, or be guilty of slander, or of
hatred.

It was the individual soul that the Divinely commissioned preachers were aiming at and seeking for.
They knew that, if the doctrine purified and perfected the soul of one man, it would be irresistible.
It would extend its influence to other souls, because
it would show, beyond all possibility of doubting,
that it could bring the life of God into human living
— and a doctrine that can do this must be true.
If the man who had stolen all his life could be
brought to cease from stealing; — if — though at a
wide remove from this man — the one who had

never been tender-hearted could be made kind and
forgiving, Paul knew that his work and mission
would be accomplished. It is so everywhere and
in all ages. The mightiest influence of Christianity
in the city or town where you reside, my friend, or in
the one where I am living, is not to be found in any
benevolent organisation, or mission work, or even
in any pastor's ministrations and efforts more truly
than it is in the simple daily life of some individual
man, prominent before the entire community, who
is, in the expressive language of the Scriptures,
known and read of all men as a true Christian —
a man whose faith works by love, and purifies the
heart — a man who in every recess and corner and
secret place of all his being lives the life which he
professes.

The words of the Apostle may seem to the reader
whose eye and thought pass quickly over them, or
by whom the depth below the surface is not seen, to
move only in the outward sphere — the sphere of
action. Do not continue to do what you have been
doing. The man that stole is exhorted to steal no
more. It is all external. But when the mind penetrates below the surface, and gets the vision of the
origin and movement and vital power and new-creat-
ing results of the forces which were in the Apostle's
thought when he used the words, it grasps the significance of what is said, and knows that the depths
are in the internal. The man who has sinned gives
up the old sinning and puts the opposite virtue in
its place, because there is a new manhood in him;

and, as he does the one thing and the other, a force goes into the new manhood which makes it grow in strength and beauty. The inward and the outward move together. But the movement begins with the inward and ends also with the inward; and so the thoughts which the Pauline words that we have been considering bring to us are thoughts of and for the inner life.

XIII

LOVE IS THE FULFILLING OF THE LAW

He that loveth his neighbour hath fulfilled the law. For this, Thou shalt not commit adultery, Thou shalt not kill, Thou shalt not steal, Thou shalt not bear false witness, Thou shalt not covet, and if there be any other commandment, it is summed up in this word, namely, Thou shalt love thy neighbour as thyself. Love worketh no ill to his neighbour: love therefore is the fulfilment of the law. — ROMANS xiii. 8–10.

THE reader of this passage, when he views it in the light of the suggestions which it offers with respect to the Christian teaching and life, cannot fail to be impressed by the contrast presented in the two expressions which give it much of its characteristic force and emphasis — the contrast between *Thou shalt not*, and *Thou shalt*. This contrast, in one view of the matter, may be regarded as a contrast between the Old Testament system and the New. The Old Testament system dealt very largely with prohibitions as connected with special wrongs and sins. The several commands which are here cited from the great and central law itself are of this character. They together make up the entire second portion of that law, which relates to our duties to our fellow-men. We are not to kill or to steal, not to bear false witness or to covet — that is, the thought is fixed upon one or another of the things which men, and particularly the men to whom the words were originally addressed, are or were disposed to do or to feel, and each one in its turn is forbidden. It sometimes seems strange to us, as we hear the words read as the Divine law still binding, that nothing further or more comprehensive should have been added. Can it be, we say, that there is no more than this in the setting forth of human duty as connected with those about us? And so, at times, it happens that the attempt is made to find in these individual prohibitions a wider significance than the words contain, as if all that we can see in the sphere of obligation were intended to be conveyed in words which, of themselves, have so much of limitation. But this mode of dealing with the commands is one which loses sight of what they really are. They prohibit special sins and evils, and have reference to these.

The same thing is true, very largely, of the law, in its more detailed presentation, as belonging to the older revelation of it. Thou shalt not, as we may say, was the characteristic form of its expression. It was so, because of the stage of development of those to whom the teaching came. In the great progress of the Divine plan of education for the race, the men of those ages represented the period of childhood. They were to be led to right moral ideas and right moral action, as all who are at the beginning must be, in largest measure by knowing what they should not do. The *prohibition*

183

of wrong was, by the necessity of the age, the chief means of communicating the *thought of right,* and bringing men to it. The early moral systems of teaching answered, in this regard, to the Divine system. They did so, because there was not readiness as yet for what was of another order, or what moved from another starting-point. The result was, that character did not reach its highest point. It never does when the limitations of the age necessitate the limitations of the teaching, after this manner — and we are not to find fault with the men, or the system, because of what could not be expected at the time. It is those to whom much is given, of whom much will be required. The child's development is not the man's, and the method of leading the child in his moral life may fitly be different from that by which the man is led.

But the latter method is higher than the former, even as the man's development is higher. The positive system is more and greater than the negative. *Thou shalt* reaches beyond *Thou shalt not.* And here we come to the first characteristic of the Christian teaching. It is not, Thou shalt not kill, or steal, or bear false witness, but, Thou shalt love. We may look through the New Testament, and we shall find it everywhere the same. There are, indeed, prohibitions in many places within the range of its different books — and prohibitions which relate to particular and special evils. But no student of these writings, who observes what they set before him and grasps their controlling thought, can be without the impression that it is the positive

184

side of moral teaching, which is altogether prominent and everywhere the same. Whether it be
Jesus himself who speaks, or Paul, or John, the
negative sinks into comparative insignificance. The
great active force is demanded, and is called into
being by the demand. As it comes forward into
activity, it accomplishes the result. The single
prohibitions fall into the line of its working and lose
themselves in its living and transforming energy.
In this very passage, how clear and plain it is:
Thou shalt love thy neighbour as thyself. He that
loveth his neighbour hath, in that very act and fact,
fulfilled the law. All that is forbidden is included
in this one positive command. And after the
same manner in the comprehensive exhortation for
Christian life, which opens and covers the entire
practical section of the epistle from which the passage is taken, we have the words: Present your
bodies a living sacrifice, holy, acceptable to God;
and be ye transformed by the renewing of your mind.
If this exhortation is fulfilled, the opposite negative,
Be not conformed to this world, as well as every suggestion which is subordinate to it, is also fulfilled.
The power of the Christian teaching, in one aspect
of it, is in its seizing thus upon the positive element
in the moral and spiritual sphere and pressing this
upon the soul as the force for character and for
true life. Herein also is its adaptation for the
moral development of manhood, as contrasted with
childhood. It is the positive force which makes
the man. The command to do the right appeals
to the manly energies and sets them in motion. It

has life in itself in a degree and measure of which the prohibition knows nothing.

In the second place, the reader who carefully observes the passage in its negative and positive parts will notice that, while the prohibitions are of the nature of rules of living in special lines, the positive command takes hold of a great principle. Love is the controlling power of the soul. When once implanted within the soul, it applies its force wherever it needs to be applied. This is strikingly manifest in the matters of which the writer is speaking in these verses. They refer to specific wrongs inflicted by one man upon another. How shall they be prevented and the tendency towards them be overcome? Not by forbidding them, one after another, as if this were the main thing to be done, says the New Testament teaching, but by bringing a principle of life to bear upon all action and feeling as between man and man. The law in its relation to one's fellow man is fulfilled by love, for the simple and sufficient reason that love does *no ill* to the fellow man. Love must, for this reason, cover and include within itself every prohibition of the doing of particular evil. It does no ill, because it pervades life and character everywhere. It accomplishes its end also, because as a positive force it excludes the desire to do evil — overcoming, at the very centre of character, the source of evil action by establishing itself as the source of good.

It is interesting to observe — and this is of the very essence of the Gospel — how Jesus, in His

186

teaching, everywhere turns the thought of His hearers from the outward act to the inward thought and feeling. The sin itself, He says, in referring to these very commands of the law which Paul here cites, is not to be discovered in the mere action, but rather behind and beneath it. It lies in the thought or desire of the soul which prompts the act. If this desire and thought be made right, all danger of the committing of the act is at once removed. Put love at the centre, and the work is complete. After a similar manner, He declares to the scribe who asked Him, as if there were higher and lower commands in the law, which commandment was first, that love is the first and all-inclusive thing enjoined by God. So also, He calls upon His most immediate and intimate disciples, along their course of life with Him and especially at the end, to let love abide in their hearts, and bids them, for the future, in their separation from Him, to love one another.

It is remarkable also how Jesus — even as Paul does here — when He was dealing with those to whom the Old Testament law was familiar, seized upon those thoughts and sentences of the Old Testament in which the deepest or widest meaning, as yet not fully apprehended, lay, and threw the light of great principles upon them. Thou shalt love thy neighbour as thyself — which had been limited in its application, and only half understood in its life-power — became, as Jesus used the words, and as Paul used them in imitation of Him, the summation of all that God would ask of men in

their relations to each other. Love avoids all evil
and urges to all good, and thus there can be nothing greater in the commandments than this, and
nothing that reaches beyond this.

The same thing is evident in the other great
matter of the law — the relation of man to God
Himself. The various duties and services, which
the Jewish system asked for in its training of the
people for what was far off in the future time, were
only manifestations of the loving spirit, or means of
bringing the mind and heart into nearness to God.
When they sank into outward and formal service, or
lost their deepest significance as duties by becoming spiritless and perfunctory, the educating force,
and the very life itself, passed out of them. So far
as they were counted as *so much doing attended by
so much result*, and the saving of the soul became a
mere reward of outward action, the divine element
in the system gave place to the human, and the
true righteousness was unknown. So plain is it
that the real vitality and living power of the older
system were wholly in the central force of love.

But it was Jesus who made this central force
known in all its significance. By His teaching the
first part of the law was filled with love, even as
was the second part; and, in the words, Thou shalt
love the Lord thy God with all thy heart, was found
the summation of all the prohibitions of the law —
to worship no other gods, to make no graven image,
not to take the Divine name in vain; and not only
this, but of all positive duty and all holy feeling
towards the Divine Father. The answer to the

scribe, which involved the statement of love to God and man, contained in itself the substance of the Christian teaching. There is, there can be, no other commandment greater than these.

Thus — as in the former case, where *Thou shalt not* precedes, and at length gives way to, *Thou shalt* — the Divine movement here again is in the line of education. The rules are for the early time, as they are, ever and everywhere, for childhood. The principles which include and pervade the rules, and which become the living force for character, are made known, and brought to bear upon the soul in their true influence, when the early time gives way to the later and childhood passes into manhood. We are not therefore — if we would be right-minded in our thinking — to find fault with or misjudge the earlier system, or the men who lived under it, as if God could not have been dealing with them to the end of righteousness, or leading them, according to the possibilities of the age indeed, yet really, to the attainment of it. But above all, we are not to misapprehend the significance and privilege and power of that system and teaching under which we ourselves live. The Christian doctrine has its meaning in a life-principle, and its power is found where its meaning is.

The careful reader, who considers these verses, will also see in them the suggestion that the life-principle, according to the Christian teaching, is expected to work in the life in a reasonable and natural way. *As thyself* is set, in the command, as the measure of the love to a fellow-man. And this expression is defined and limited, as it were, by the following words, Love worketh no ill to his neighbour; therefore love is the fulfilment of the law. The man who comes under the true influence of the teaching is *so far* to love, *as to do no evil;* to refrain from all such injury to his fellow-man as is indicated in the prohibitions of the ancient law, and from all evil of a minor character which is suggested by them, even as he would refrain from injury to himself. He is, as he turns to the positive side of the matter, to do his neighbour good as readily and earnestly as he would do himself good. The impulses of his heart, that is, as impelling to action, are not to centre in or upon himself and his own well-being, but are to move outward towards the welfare of others.

But he is not called upon in every sense, and every outlook of his life, to do for them what he does for himself. The life of each man is entrusted in a peculiar manner to his own keeping, and there must be an interest in and devotion to it, which cannot be given to any or every other life. When Jesus said to His own disciples that they should love one another as He had loved them, He did not mean that they should love every disciple with an equal love, or that the love, in any case, should absolutely equal His own. This could not have been His demand, for His power of loving was greater than theirs. He meant that, in every case, they should love according to the possibilities of their nature and condition, even as He had done. He had loved them all alike, in that He had lived to do them

190

good. He called upon them to love one another after the same manner. The meaning of the law, as interpreted by His teaching, is readiness ever to do good and unwillingness ever to do evil. It is, in a single word, love which thus moves the man always in his relation to his fellow-man.

This love — which duly regards the personal life, but continually reaches out to other lives — lifts the soul in love to Him who is higher than all. The brotherhood of men opens towards the fatherhood of God. And so, as the command which enjoins the spirit of the brotherhood carries on the man to the fulfilment of that greater command, which calls for all-controlling love towards the Divine Father, the end of all true living is secured. The life-principle is one, only with different outworkings. It pervades the soul, and inspires its movements whithersoever it turns in all its relations, and thus becomes for each and every man the complete fulfilment of the law in both of its parts. The enmity to God and man alike is done away in every manifestation of it, and it passes into an affection which, as related to the one, is more than the love to one's self — supreme and above all things; — and, as related to the other, is equal to the love to self — ever moving outward, as readily as it turns inward. The working, everywhere, is in accordance with the natural movement of the life.

In view of the thoughts which have thus been presented, let us not misunderstand what the Christian system is. We are all prone to put ourselves on the standpoint of the older teaching. As we are called to the new life, or as we go forward in it, the rules and prohibitions assume the place of prominence in our thinking. We stand just outside the gate of Christian living, and, as we look inward upon the path along which we are asked to move, we seem to see everywhere placed before us the words, Thou shalt not. These words appear to attach themselves to actions, and pleasures, and purposes for our own well-being, and plans and hopes for the earthly career. The doctrine, we say to ourselves, is a forbidding one. It denies us almost everything on which we have fixed our thoughts and desires. It penetrates everywhere, and makes life a hard service. It may perhaps be fitted for the later years, when the joy of youth and manhood come to their end, and preparation must be made for what lies beyond the boundary of this world. But we cannot listen to the call now, when life is too happy in its possibilities and enjoyments for the suffering of prohibition on every side. And so we turn back from the gate as it opens for us and refuse to obey the summons.

But all this is misapprehension. Christianity is not a negative moral system, or one that is made up of rules or prohibitions only which attend the man at every step. Its teaching is positive. The spring and power of life, which it gives, is a principle. You are invited, my friend, to take the love-principle into your soul, and let it work there. To move you to accept the invitation — the love of God as your Father, dealing tenderly with you, watching over

you always, bestowing upon you a multitude of
blessings, filling the years for you as they pass with
more and more of good, is set before your mind, to
the end that you may, if possible, see how much
greater and better He is than all other friends.
To impel you still further, the relation of all other
men — like the relation of yourself — to Him as
Father is made known, and you are awakened, if
you can be, to the grand, inspiring thought of the
great brotherhood, with common needs, and hopes,
and life. And, as uniting in Himself the Divine and
human, Jesus appears before you, according to the
Christian teaching, with His *divine example* and
His *human affection*, and asks you to become like
Him in your soul's living. The principle is implanted within you, if you will receive it, and you
are left to its working. Life now begins from a
new point — from the opposite point, as contrasted
with what you were thinking of, — and it develops
in the happiest and most natural way.

What is the working? It is the same with that
of the love-principle everywhere. It excludes the
wrong things and the evil desires, not by turning
the mind to the prohibitory command relating to
each sinful act or course of action, but by so filling
the mind with itself that the wish to do ill passes
away. It is wonderful how the Christian teaching,
with a sublime confidence, leaves the love-principle,
as it enters the disciple's soul, to itself — assured
that it will accomplish its work. It has no doubts
or fears, for it knows the transforming power which
the living principle has within it. Its outlook is ever

forward, and it sees the results in the future. And well it may have this confidence, for the love-force is the positive all-creating and all-subduing life-force. You are asked to begin the Christian life just as you would begin any other life where the love-force is the governing principle. The positive element of the life takes care of all on the negative side; and, just as far and as fast as the character grows, the hardness of giving up what is forbidden ceases, and the development becomes continuous and joyous. Look at the growth of love anywhere, and you will see that it carries all this in itself.

The Christian life has great promises, my friends. Whatever else we may do respecting it, let us not turn aside from its call, and lose its gifts, through a misapprehension of what it asks of us, and of what it offers to us as its moving power.

But our misunderstanding is not only at the beginning and while we are yet outside of the gateway. We linger often under the influence of the old ideas, after we have been long moving on in the new way of living. We think of the Christian system still as one of rules and prohibitions, and concentrate our thought upon these. *Thou shalt not* continues to be the great word of command. As the result of this we become severe in our judgment of others and, oftentimes, of ourselves, also. The prohibitions of the law are studied, perhaps, in all their minuteness as they may be made to bear upon present action, or they are extended to a sphere of conduct which they were not intended to cover. If another violates them in any measure, as they

are thus extended and applied, we declare him to
be losing sight of duty or wandering off from the
Christian path. If we find ourselves failing at times,
even in matters the wrong of which is questionable,
we become anxious for our own well-being. We
move downward or backward from the Christian
idea to the idea of the old system as the Jews of
the time of Jesus understood it — losing sight of
its truest and deepest significance.

The revelation of the Gospel was other than this.
It was the revelation of the love-principle as the
transforming life-power. It was the revelation, in
all clearness, of what had not been apprehended
before — the revelation of God as the Father of the
great brotherhood of men, and of love as the uniting force binding the membership of the brotherhood to one another and all alike to God. If the
love which answers the demands of the relationship
in which the man stands dwells in his heart, he can
be trusted in his action. The love itself fulfils the
law. Whatever he may do while love is triumphant within him, and while there is in the act, or
the feeling which prompts it, no inconsistency with
love, he may do rightly. If love be thus all-controlling, all questions will settle themselves, and the
man may be where he will with the true life still
abiding in all its strength. The system of rules,
and of these only, has passed for him into a system
of principle, and he is free with the freedom that
is given by Christ.

And here is the educating power for manhood.
It is easier, in one sense, to be in the childhood

state, and to have rules set for us at every step, so that we know just what we may, and may not, do. Life needs comparatively little thought or decision or resolution, when it is adjusted thus. But manhood is not appointed to be without thought, and decision, and resolution. These are essential elements pertaining to it, as distinguished from childhood. The man is designed for principles, not rules — to take them as the governing force of life — to apply them in every critical moment of thought and action. The responsibility of decision continually develops the manly power.

And so Christianity works upon us, and in us, by imposing upon our lives this responsibility. It deals with us and treats us, thus, in the manliest way. It tells us, at its first meeting with our souls, of what we know in some measure from our own experience — that love is the great working force for character. It reveals to us — what is beyond our limited human knowledge, but what we might hope to be true from what we see of the human soul — that the same force is that which brings us into nearest relation to God and transforms us into His likeness. It points us to God Himself, as having the same life-force in His own Divine life, and as ever sending forth His love to those who love Him. It thus offers to us its great gift and bids us take it, with its word of command, Thou shalt love God supremely, and thy fellow-man as thyself. And then, when we accept its offer and yield to its bidding, it tells us to go on our way rejoicing. Love, it assures us, will answer all questions, prompt all actions, control all life,

reject all evil, take to itself all good. Let it always
abide in the soul and do its own work. This is
what it says — and along the way, and at the end,
it brings its peaceful message to the soul in the
words, Love is the fulfilment of the law.

I commend to you, once more, my young friends,
the Christian message and the Christian teaching.
If you will receive into your souls the great life-
principle which is presented to you for your acceptance, it will become for you an ever-working power
— whose working will overcome evil as the days
and years pass. It will continually develop largest
and grandest manhood, and will bring beautiful and
peaceful life for all the future. The gift which
Christianity offers is a great one. It will become
greater to your thought, the more you know of it in
your own personal experience. Let your mind rest
upon it, and upon all that it bears with itself.

XIV

LIKENESS TO CHRIST THE BEGINNING AND END OF OUR SONSHIP TO GOD

Beloved, now are we children of God, and it is not yet made manifest what we shall be. We know that if he shall be manifested, we shall be like him; for we shall see him even as he is.— I JOHN iii. 2.

THE writer of these words, at the time of his writing them, had had a very peculiar experience as related to the Christian truth and life. He had been summoned very soon after the beginning of the ministry of Jesus to the office and work of the Apostleship and had, accordingly, had the most abundant opportunities to learn from Jesus what He had to teach on every subject connected with His mission to the world and with the Divine revelation. With a mind wonderfully adapted to receive the truth and ever ready to penetrate as far as possible into its deepest meaning, he must, as we cannot doubt, have sought by questioning, by continued reflection, by careful study of the working of the truth in his own mind and heart, and in the minds and hearts of his fellow disciples, and by every means within his power, to enter into the full possession of what he had heard from the lips of his Master. A long period had now passed since the Master's death,

and, with the progress of these years, the more outward communion, as it might be called, had changed
into the more inward one. But he had meditated
upon the truth, and in his soul had drawn near to
the source of truth, and had dwelt in thought upon
the development of his own interior life, and had
looked intently backward to the old experience, now
become the richest of all memories, and forward to
the great mysterious future ever drawing nearer to
himself. He was, at the date of his writing, almost
at the end of life here, and almost at the beginning
of life hereafter — when the hopes and dreams of
what is beyond most fill the soul.

It cannot but be a matter of interest to think of
these words of the epistle as revealing what one who
had been so intimately related to Jesus, and who was
so near to the promised reunion with Him, had
learned of the future life in its connection with the
present, and what he had not learned.

Of the special experiences of the future life he
had learned nothing. Two things in the teaching of
Jesus, and His intercourse with the Apostles, impress
us as very remarkable, I think, when we study the
Gospel history in relation to this matter. The first
is, that, although His teaching was continually of
the things belonging to the soul's life, and thus
moved oftentimes, as if by necessity, on the borders
of the hereafter, He seems never to have lifted the
veil for a moment, or given the Apostles even a
passing vision of the things which lay behind it.
He told them nothing which could be wrought

by their subsequent reflection into the semblance of knowledge. The other thing is, if possible, more strange and striking, to my own mind, than this. It is, that they did not press Him with questions on this matter, and try to gain from Him thereby something which might satisfy the eager inquiries and strong desires of their own minds. There must have been, as it would seem, some mysterious influence in His presence and character, and some wonderful concentration of His words, in all His intercourse with them, upon duty and service and the inner life, which awed them into a silence almost like His own with reference to the unseen world. A similar silence, if we may so express it, seems to have continued with them and stilled their questionings, after they were left to their own thoughts, and when the revelations of the Spirit came to them, to lead them into the truth.

How often, and with how much interest, a mind like that of the writer of this epistle, it would seem, must have dwelt upon the *circumstances* and *conditions* under which his own character might grow into a higher than earthly completeness in another state of existence. So we should say to ourselves, before we read the record of his thoughts. But when we read it, we find him telling us no more of these things than we, who never saw the Lord and talked with Him, can tell one another; and even the questions which rise so often in our minds seem to have been lost for him in the peaceful and loving confidence in which he moved forward in the daily service of God. We *are* children of God, he says, but what we *shall be* is not yet made manifest. He says this as calmly as if he had never dreamed of the possibility of answering the question respecting the future; as if he had never seen a messenger from the other world who knew everything relating to the life there; almost as if the details of that life had been beyond the limits of his thought.

That he had thought, however, of the life beyond is manifest from many passages in his writings, and even from the one before us. It is manifest, also, from what his writings reveal to us of himself. A meditative, self-contemplative man, such as he was — to whom the growth of mind and character is the most important of all things in the world, and who has an intense interest in the working and movement of his own mind and character — cannot make the present life the boundary of his thinking. As he sees the wonderful capabilities of his soul, and the hindrances and imperfections which beset it here, he must go out in his hopes and imagination to a more perfect state, in which the growth will be an unending one. And so it doubtless was in his case; and he came to deep conviction, and even to assurance, as he meditated. Of the details and precise conditions of the future he knew nothing indeed. He was content to wait for this knowledge until all should be revealed. But that a better and higher life was before him he was well-assured, and what would be its great characteristic, and the source of its blessedness, he knew with a knowledge that was like the realisation of the blessedness in his own soul. It is not yet made manifest what we shall be;

but we know that when He shall be manifested, we shall be like Him.

Let us look somewhat more closely at what this knowledge was, and how it grew within him. The foundation of the thought of the verses seems to be in the expression: children of God. The Johannean idea of the child-relationship to God is that of likeness to Him in character. As the human soul comes into union and fellowship with God, a new principle is implanted within it, which corresponds with that by which the Divine life itself is guided. The entrance of this principle makes the man God's child. This entrance is secured by faith, which is the basis and essential element of spiritual union. We may believe that the Apostle gained this conception, so far as it was peculiar to himself, from his own experience. We cannot suppose that, when he first came to Jesus and gave himself up to friendship with Him, there was any great crisis or violent overturning in his life, as there was, for example, in the case of Paul. His nature and his earlier life were of a different sort. He was a man of thoughtfulness, far more exclusively than Paul was, and he had turned already with willingness to the teachings of John the Baptist and had, not improbably, been from the beginning a follower of the light so far as it had come to him from the Old Testament. When he found in Jesus the promised messenger from heaven, therefore, he simply sat at His feet and learned of Him. As the Divine influence passed from the Master to the disciple, faith

became to him immediately a working and transforming principle. It was the power of a new life
springing up in his soul. Spiritually, he found
himself to be what he had not been before. His
mind and heart had been born again. The life
within him had only to *grow from this beginning*,
in order to become perfect. He saw, as at the time
of his writing he looked backward from his far-
advanced age, that it had been growing steadily,
and that it was now much deeper and larger and
stronger than in the first days; — but it was still
the same thing, and it had not yet reached its highest possibility. We cannot wonder that it seemed
to him to be like the natural life, which comes into
being by a force outside of itself, and then only
goes on and develops, under all the influences sur-
rounding it and through all the powers within it,
until it reaches the fulness of its growth. He was
a child of God on the first day of the revelation of
Jesus to his soul. He was a child of God still,
though half a century had passed away, and what he
had gained seemed almost too great to be measured.
The change which had taken place was only the natural progress of a life in its appropriate conditions.

The influence also, which had been most powerful in causing the growth, and had been working
constantly through all the years, was the same that
had originated the life within him. As he saw
Jesus, and heard Him speak of Himself and of the
truth, he believed, and thus entered into fellowship
with God. The inner life of Jesus infused itself
into his own inner life, as he communed with Him

in the daily intercourse of the time that followed, even to the day of the crucifixion. How evident it is, that in his association with Jesus there was realised a union in which the character of the one absorbed into itself, in a wonderful degree, the character of the other, and the two persons became one, as we say, not only because they were closely joined together in affection, but especially because there was a common life-principle filling their souls; a life-principle given forth by the one and received as the source of life by the other. And, after their separation by reason of the death of Jesus, the Apostle grew in his soul's living by the remembrance and study of what Jesus was.

No reader of his Gospel and first Epistle can question this. Indeed, so manifest are the evidences which establish the fact, that some, who have not appreciated the striking proofs of historic truthfulness in his narrative in the Gospel, have thought the whole of it to be but the result of musings and reflections on what the author had learned of Jesus from the other Gospel stories. If it be true of any person in the world's history, that he developed gradually into what he was in his inmost character by the seeing of another's character and life, this was true in the highest degree of John in relation to Jesus. He sat at Jesus' feet; he gathered into himself the lessons of His history; he contemplated Him as the perfect man who was to be imitated by other men, if they desired perfection; he looked to Him as revealing and possessing within Himself that life of God which is light, and in which there is no darkness at all; and, as he looked, he became more and more like Him.

Now he was conscious of all this. He knew that he was, and had been for long years past, a child of God, and that he had been growing in his character, from the first days, into the Divine likeness through his seeing the Lord Jesus with the eye of his mind and soul. But if he knew this with reference to the past, what did the knowledge bear with it respecting the future? Nothing, indeed, as to the particular circumstances, or employments, or conditions of growth, or other details of the new state of being upon which he should enter. Of all this he knew no more as he came to the closing day of his Christian life on earth than he had known on the day of its beginning. But one thing his experience had placed within his knowledge: — that, as his life had grown, in some measure, into the likeness of God's life through the sight of Jesus in the past—a partial and limited vision, at the best, because of the limitations of the earthly state, — it would grow into the perfect likeness of that life when he should come to see Him in all the glory of His being, precisely as He is. The promise of Jesus, on the last evening of His life, had assured him that the time was coming when He would be manifested. The history of his own inner life had made known to him all the rest — had made it certain, beyond a doubt or a fear, that when Jesus should be manifested he would be like Him; and this because of the more perfect vision. I shall see

Him as He is, and His life will become mine. The influence of the Divine friendship, which begins in this world, will continue forever — ever penetrating and transforming and glorifying the soul which has once trusted itself and its future to the love and care of that friendship.

The verses declare to us that every believer has this child-relationship to God, which the writer is himself conscious of possessing. If the life of the soul is the development of a principle which is implanted through a Divine influence, the life must, of course, come into being at the very moment of the implanting of the principle. The child-relationship begins from birth. The Apostle addresses all the members of the Christian body, to whom he wrote, with the words before us, and declares them to be true of all alike. He claims nothing of privilege or blessing for himself as distinguished from them, and nothing apparently for himself, at this later period of his life, beyond what he saw that he had fully possessed in the hour when he first believed. There had been growth since then, but no change of life-principle. What is involved in his words, therefore, both for the present and the future, belongs to all — to the youngest Christian as truly as to the oldest.

It is also worthy of notice that — when he suggests the evidences or indications of the new life — they are those which the youngest, as well as the oldest, may find within himself. The two evidences which are brought before us are the indwelling in

the soul of something which the world — the un-
believing, sinful world — does not know; and the
out-going of the soul's desire after purity; that is, a
life-principle, and a life-movement, both of which are
marked by a likeness to Christ. The reality of the
life is not determined by *the strength* of this principle,
or *the secured results* of this movement, but by *their
existence* in the soul. The man who is conscious of
an impulse towards right living therefore, as a follower of Christ, which he did not have in former
years, or which he did not have yesterday it may
be, and who is ready to act in accordance with it in
a loving, trustful, childlike way, may know that he
is now a child of God — just beginning his new life
perhaps, but yet a true child of the Divine family.
And the work for to-morrow, for the coming years,
for the life-time, is only to grow towards the fulness
of Christ himself.

What a simple and beautiful thing it is, as we view
it in the light of the experience which is revealed to
us in these verses. Likeness to Christ is that which
enters the soul at the hour when the act of faith
opens to the Christian the new career. Likeness to
Christ is the consummation at the end, when the
earthly living has passed into the heavenly, and the
imperfection of the one has become the perfectness
of the other. And all the way from the beginning
to the ending, this likeness is the result of a study
of Christ's character — the lessons and influences of
IIis life transforming themselves into the principles
and actions of the disciple's life. This is what every
believer may know: — that he is to-day a child of

God's household, and that, therefore, he will be like
Him as He is revealed in Christ; — that the life-
principle unknown by the world and the life-movement of pure desire will, in the day when He is
manifested, have their complete and victorious
power over every faculty of the soul. As the
imperfect sight of the present has occasioned the
partial resemblance, which he now sees within himself, the seeing Him in the future *as He is* will make
the resemblance forever complete.

This is the wonderful thing about the child-relationship, and the thing which makes it, in a pure
and thoughtful and noble household, so great a
blessing for the life. As we closely observe a family
history, how remarkable it is. As soon as the child
begins his development, he shows to all about him
— perhaps unconsciously to himself — a sort of
peculiar life-principle which came to him from his
father or his mother, and which makes him different
in his qualities, his mental growth, his peculiar ex-
hibitions of virtue and character, from the children
of other families. The life-movement is along the
line of the life-principle ; and, as he grows up to maturity, he bears on the ancestral character from the
past generations towards the future. How is it that he
grows thus? Not by rules and precepts which are
laid down for him. Not by a paternal command
that requires him to imitate his parents. Not even
by laboured efforts on his own part to be like those
whom he loves in his home. These things, especially
the one last mentioned, have their influence on his

living. But — more than all these things, and nearer to the centre of life's forces — he grows by *seeing his parents as they are.* He lives in their presence, as he passes from childhood to maturity, and their life becomes his life. If they have Christian piety filling the atmosphere of their home, the same piety comes so gradually, and gently, and sweetly, into his soul, that he is often unconscious, and they are also, of the hour when the new power begins to bear sway over his soul. If they are intelligent and thoughtful, he grows into their likeness. If generosity, and kindness, and purity, and peace, and love are in their hearts, the years pass on a little way, and we see the same virtues taking strong hold upon his character and life. The religious atmosphere makes the child religious; the thoughtful atmosphere makes him thoughtful. So we often say; and sometimes we wonder at the result, because so little of what we call positive effort seems to have been put forth. But the child *sees* the *inner life* of those whose child he is, and his life, in after years, is like theirs *because he has seen it.* And how little, as his course begins and the days pass by him, he realises what is going on within himself! How dim is his vision of what is to follow in the result! He simply goes through his daily employments and amusements, his pleasures and his duties, — what is before him, he cannot tell. But he is *seeing* a pure life and *breathing* a thoughtful and Christian air, and, by and by, the future unfolds to him with the richest blessing which this world can give.

Such also, and after the same manner, is the child-relationship to God, only He is infinitely purer and better than we are, and infinitely nearer, we may almost say, to our souls than we can be to one another. To see Him, is the education of the soul. To see Him as He is, is to be like Him. The message, which the Divine messenger, whom this writer had known in the past years and with whom he hoped soon to be re-united, brought to His followers, was of this child-relationship and its promise.

What the Apostle did not understand, therefore, because it was not yet made manifest, — and what we, like him, cannot yet know, — was only the peculiar circumstances of the remoter future; the special conditions of the life beyond the veil. The place of living would change, and what the change would be, precisely, had never been revealed to him, as it has not been to us. But this is a comparatively small matter. It belongs, as we may say, to the externals and the accidental only. The *great reality* is *the child life* as related to God, which came into your soul or mine at some past moment, as it came to the Apostle in his early manhood. That life takes hold upon the eternal future and, whatever may be the imperfection of its growth thus far, so it be really existing, it bears within itself the promise of an all-glorious perfectness. It is not yet made manifest what we shall be, but we know that when He shall be manifested, we shall be like Him; for we shall see Him even as He is.

It is not strange, then, that as this writer saw and felt all this, he rose into a lofty conception of the power of faith, and thought of the life that begins with faith as never having a sight or taste of death. Death, to the believer, is simply the passing from the partial seeing to the seeing Him as He is. The sadness and sorrowfulness of its meaning are lost, and it ceases to be itself. The life becomes one and perpetual, now here and after a season there, but ever more full of light and blessedness because ever more in the likeness of His life.

XV

THE PEACE OF CHRIST A RULING POWER

Let the peace of Christ rule in your hearts, to the which also ye were called in one body; and be ye thankful.
COLOSSIANS iii. 15.

THESE words have a striking and peculiar character which is fitted to arrest the attention of the thoughtful reader. There is seemingly a strange significance in themselves — what can they mean? There is something even more remarkable, if possible, in their position and prominence — what is the thought which they press upon the mind? That peace should dwell in our hearts; that it should be within them a power for calmness or comfort; that it should be as a guard keeping the thoughts in restfulness — all this is in accordance with its nature, we say, and the suggestion of these things by the Christian teachers is clearly harmonious with the doctrine which they teach. But when we think of a ruling power, is not something more active and forceful needed in the soul's life, we ask, and does not Christianity so represent it? Love, with its propelling energy, may well be spoken of as such a power. So may faith, with its inspiration and its hold upon the invisible. So again may hope, with its confident and courageous outlook towards the future. But peace is quiet, and still, and peaceful — how can it rule; especially, how can it rule in the midst of that struggle of the soul, in which the old evil forces, all-controlling in the past, are to be put away and destroyed, and the new forces of the new life are to be made victorious?

In this remarkable passage, however, peace is set forth as governing, rather than love itself, although love is in the very same passage called the bond of perfectness and is urged as above all things else that are mentioned — and even more than this, the exhortation respecting peace is added to all the other exhortations, as if in the fulfilment of this were the consummation and completeness of that which was demanded and desired by the Christian teaching. It is as if the writer had said to his readers: In order that you may so set your mind on the things that are above as to find and possess for yourselves the life which is in Christ and God, and may thus put off the old man with his doings, and put on the new man who is renewed after the image of Him that created him, you must let the peace of Christ rule in your hearts. This is that to which you were called. This is that for which, as you realise it in your own experience, you may be most truly thankful. The very strangeness of the words, as they first present themselves to our thought, may appropriately lead us to consider them more attentively. Such an attentive consideration, I think, will give us a clearer apprehension of their meaning and, at the same time, a sense of their fitness and truthfulness.

The peace here spoken of is not mere quietness of spirit, or evenness in the movement of the life and its powers. Were it this alone, it could hardly with justice be described, or demanded, as a *governing force*. And yet even such peace is no insignificant element in the matter of developing character or of accomplishing a man's best work. We may look about us, and we shall see that those in whom the mental or moral faculties are constantly operating without friction or fretfulness, are the men who, at least when other things are equal, are the most successful. The mind or soul which is not in peace — which is disturbed by anxiety or doubt or fear or foreboding — loses a part, often a large part, of its energy in connection with these things. It must overcome them, if they are to be overcome, by using a portion of its forces in a struggle with their power or, in case it does not resist them, it must of necessity abide with half of its life among them, not escaping from their dominion into the full liberty of its own joyous action. The evenly, easily moving mind on the other hand, tied down by no fetters, and freely working by the exercise of all its faculties, is ready for each new effort. It may concentrate itself upon that to which it is called at any moment, and may command itself wholly for the task assigned. It has nothing behind, or apart, to hinder its progress, but is able to pass on with its full strength from what has been accomplished to

what is to be effected in the early future. So too
with the soul. It is the anxiety about the old
things and the dwelling among them that restrain
the soul, oftentimes, in the putting forth of all its
efforts for the one end of gaining for itself the new
things. Character develops slowly, because the
development is with but a part of the forces. The
man is *divided*, according to the expressive word
which the New Testament writers use to set forth
the idea of anxiety. He is drawn this way and that
way, and is not *one within himself.* He cannot forget the past in such a sense as to give himself
entirely to the pressing forward towards that which
is before him. He fails therefore, or half-way fails,
where he might otherwise succeed. There must be,
in this sense as it would seem, even a certain
dominion of peace within the soul, or the end is not
perfectly secured. If the peace is not strictly, and
in the full meaning of the word, the ruling force, it
unites itself with the ruling force and helps it everywhere and always. We realise this, all of us, for
ourselves so soon as we begin to study the experiences of our inmost life — and the more so, as we
advance along the line of the years. We learn the
lesson and understand the truth, whether we know
the peacefulness as our own personal possession or
not. The case is one where the absence or the
presence of the thing desired tells the same story,
though it tells it from a different starting-point and
in a different way. And I believe that the thoughtful man, in his estimate of the elements of his real
life-power, as to their relative importance, will often

question which is of greater value — the energy
that *impels* him to *action*, or the peacefulness
which enables the energy to have its *full impulse
unrestrained.*

But the peace to which our verse from the
Apostle's letter refers is something more than this
quietness or evenness, of which we are speaking.
It is called the peace of Christ, and is counted
among the powers of Christian living. It is an
element of Christ's life which is imparted to His
followers' lives, and is to be apprehended, in its
significance, only as we see what it was for Him.
The expression itself seems to be suggested by the
words which Christ used in His talk with the disciples on the last evening before His death. Peace
I leave with you, He said to them at that time; my
peace I give unto you. And then He added the
impressive sentence: Not as the world giveth, give
I unto you. It was not a worldly peace in any
sense of the word, which He would impart to them
— not a peace even which might, by any possibility,
enter the mind or the heart apart from Himself, and
might, by reason of the calm and even movement
of the life which it should secure, add to all the
powers and successes of the man to whom it came.
It was above and beyond this — a possession belonging only to Himself, which should be for His
disciples what it was for Him and which they could
see in the manifestation of its nature and its effi-
cacy, if they would, as they looked upon Him *at
that hour.* If they thus looked, they would recognise it as an active, not a mere passive thing — a

thing of force and energy, which *could rule* and *was ruling* the life of the man. If they looked more carefully and more continuously, they would discover it as fundamental to all His living — as true and controlling a life-power as love itself.

The hour when Jesus thus used the words in speaking to the eleven was the darkest hour in His career. It was the closing hour in a long succession of dark ones, in which His soul had been tested and tried to its deepest depths. It was the critical hour towards which all the past had been moving, and the movement —to human thought, at least — seemed to have been towards failure and loss. What did the peace which He then called His peace do for Him — what was it within Him? It was surely something more than mere calmness of spirit, which kept Him at rest among the doubts and dangers that surrounded His life and His cause. It was this, but it was, at the same time, much more than this. It was something which gathered into itself all His far-reaching thought of the Divine plan for the Divine kingdom — all His willing obedience to His Father's will, whithersoever that will should call Him — all His fixedness of resolve to carry out the idea and purpose of His earthly mission — all His heroism of self-sacrifice, even to the consummation of His sufferings — all the mightiness of His power to be and to do at the end that for which He had been sent at the beginning. It was thus inseparable from every force that was discoverable within Him. It regulated all these forces, and held them in their true adjustment to one an-

other. It directed their activity in accordance with
the demand of the hour, and so imparted its own
influence that they moved harmoniously. It became, in and of itself, an inspiration and life-giving
power for all the forces. We see its sovereign
authority and its impelling energy in His words of
every sort during those last days.

How wonderful those words were as they turned
towards one and another person or towards one or
another experience. The word of prayer addressed
to the Father, Shall I say, save me from this hour
— no — it was for this cause that I came unto this
hour. The word to the disciples, That the world
may know that, as the Father hath given me commandment, even so I do, arise, let us go hence.
The word to Peter, Thinkest thou that I cannot
pray unto my Father, and he shall even now send
me more than twelve legions of angels, but how
then should the scriptures be fulfilled, that so it
must be? The word to the Roman governor, Thou
wouldest have no power at all against me except it
were given thee from above. The word to the Jewish high-priest, Henceforth ye shall see the Son of
Man sitting at the right hand of power, and coming
on the clouds of heaven. The word to the scorn-
ful sceptic, who had a half-compassionate contempt
for him, Every one that is of the truth heareth
my voice. The word to His mother, Woman, behold thy son, and to the disciple, behold thy
mother. The word to the sorrowing eleven, I
have overcome the world. The word for Himself, I am not alone, because the Father is with

me. The word for His work and His life, It is finished.

These words, in their appropriateness to each moment — giving expression, at one moment, to a sense of power; at another, to a sublime confidence in the future; at another, to an assurance of victory already secured; at another, to a consciousness of union with the Father; at another, to a tender affection for those whom He was to leave behind Him and a thoughtfulness for their coming necessity; at another, to a ready submission to the will of God, and the final summons of duty; and, at the last, to a deep and satisfying conviction that all things pertaining to the great mission had been accomplished — were all governed and sent forth by the peace within Him. They answered, each and every one of them, to that peace. They would have been impossible without it. They sprang forth from it and rose out of it, as naturally as love comes forth from the loving soul, or truth from the truthful soul — and after the same manner. The inspiration of them all was in it, as it held them all in its power and ruled them all.

The Christian believer is an imitator of Christ and a recipient of His spirit. The peace therefore which is given to him from the Master will become for him, and will work within him, that which it was and wrought in the Master's life. It will have dominion throughout the whole sphere of the inward man. It will hold all things under its authority and will send forth its guiding and impelling force into every emotion, and every resolution, and every

action, and every consecration, which pertain to
him as a man, ever and everywhere moving him to
the noblest living in all the heroism, whether of
suffering or of triumph, which he may know in his
career.

It is interesting to look into the Apostle's thought,
as he sets forth the development of the individual
life in the passage from which our verse is taken,
and to see how the ruling peace is related to the
whole of it from its beginning to its ending. The
ruling peace settles all questions, directs all forces,
turns the mind whither it should turn, establishing
it also in fixedness there, and brings to a gradual
realisation the completeness of the true life. In the
conflict between anger and kindness — if we study
the details which he gives — or between falsehood
and truth, or between evil desire and holy purpose,
or between the old impulses and powers, any or all
of them, and the new, it determines which should
and must prevail. In the work of putting off the
old man and putting on the new man, it at once
adjusts the soul to its task and points to it the
·right way. In the matter of the seeking of the
things that are above, it gives inspiration, by showing that itself abides in, and in connection with,
those things. In the sphere of the promise of the
future, it strengthens confidence by imparting of
its own calm assurance that the promise will be
realised. The word which the Apostle uses to express the *ruling* idea is a peculiar one, as to the
central thought of which there has been somewhat
of questioning — some holding that the arbitrating

or judging function of a ruling authority, as in a
conflict between opposite forces, is prominent; and
others, that the special meaning is that of the ruler's
bestowal of reward, at the end of a contest, or
perhaps that of his direction or guidance of a
course, or a struggle; and others, again, that all
limitation of significance passes away, and that the
word is only a forceful one expressing the idea of
governing in the widest and largest sense. But the
ruling peace, as we trace its influence and power in
the life-process which he opens before us, satisfies all these meanings, and moves, as we may say,
in its significance through them all, as it directs and
controls the living forces.

Let us turn our thought now towards our own
personal experience, and see how interesting the
thought becomes to us there. There are times when
every Christian believer knows within himself the
presence, not only of a peaceful spirit, giving calmness, but of a ruling peace, taking the life under its
authority. These times are passing seasons with
most of us, indeed, but they continue long enough to
teach us their lesson and reveal to us some measure
of the truth. How quickly, as they come, do we
realise that we are, for the hour, adjusted in our
thinking and purpose to the Divine plan, and how
soon after their coming do all thoughts and impulses
place themselves in readiness for the word of
authority which the ruling power may speak. That
authoritative word holds in restraint, or sets in
motion, according as the movement of the plan
demands. The man therefore acts with the right

forces at the right moment, and the acting and resting forces alike, in peaceful adjustment to each
other, serve the great end to be secured. I look
within myself, the Christian says at such a season,
and behold, the old doubting and disquietude have
passed away. I listen for the inward voice, which
becomes to me as the Divine voice, and in obedience
to it I put forth the energy which the hour calls for.
I lose anxiety for distant results, and centre my
thought upon present duty and service. I strive to
be kindly when the call for kindness comes, and
self-sacrificing when it comes with the summons for
sacrifice, and heroic when the duty involves heroism.
I find my powers at each moment, and in answer
to each call, in readiness or order for their work.
They are so because peace is the reigning power,
and hence they cannot contend against each other,
or usurp each other's places, or move out of
harmony with the common purpose of good. How
beautiful life seems to be for the moment — how
right it seems ! Character takes a new starting-point
for its growth and development. Manhood becomes
larger and nobler, as in the image of Christ and of
God.

The season passes indeed, and we fall backward
into the old condition, but the lesson is not lost
altogether, nor are we altogether what we were before. The entrance way for peace in the after days
opens more easily into our souls, than it did long
ago. The experience, when it has ceased as a present
experience, lingers with us as a testimony and as a
bright vision, and, in some hour of new impulse, we

find it in its reality once more. This is the process and progress — even as the Apostle recognised it — and, as the years pass, we know within ourselves what he taught and urged upon his readers. The ruling peace becomes to our thought and our life more and more the central force of all forces, taking love and humility and forgiveness and courage and every virtue of the manly Christian life under its sway, and making them, in their harmonious development, triumphant in the character. We see in this ruling peace the power which realises for us what it realised for the Master, and know it joyfully as the Master's peace given to His disciples.

We see also — through our own experience — the truth and fitness of the statement which the Apostle adds to his exhortation. Unto this peace, he says to each one of his readers, you were called. For this reason, let it ever abide within you and rule over you. The calling of God, according to the strictest sense of the words — as we find it represented in many passages of the New Testament writings — is a calling to participation in the Divine kingdom, its life and its rewards as they shall manifest themselves in the future. But that life and those rewards rest upon, and consist in, what the soul, by means of the call and under the influences of the kingdom, possesses in itself. To make the soul what it should be, is the purpose of God. To give it the characteristics of the kingdom, and make its life to move in the atmosphere of the kingdom's life, is that for which He is, first of all, working in

the carrying out of His plan of love. The soul that
is right will secure the blessedness. And so the
call directs itself to the end of the soul's right living
— to the impelling of the soul towards the sphere
where right living finds its natural home. That
sphere, as we have already seen, is the sphere of
peace. The right life is the life which is adjusted
properly to every duty and every privilege. The life
governed and guided by the peace of Christ is the
life which is thus adjusted. The Christian is thus
as truly called to *peace*, as he is called to *heaven*.
He is called to peace, we may fitly say, *because* he is
called to heaven; for the heavenly life is but the
experience, in its ever-continuing fulness, of that
happy state of the soul in which Christ's peace is
the ruling force.

The exhortation after this manner answers to the
call, and finds its legitimate and fundamental reason
in it. To be called to peace, and to live outside of
its sphere, is a contradiction at the very centre of
the life. To be called to it as the ruling element
and principle in the soul's developing of itself for
the kingdom in the future, and not to give it dominion over all things else, in the progress of that
development, is to deny the call at the outset, and
to lose the richness of its reward at the end.

But the exhortation takes into itself the force of
an additional reason beyond the one just mentioned.
Ye were called unto peace as individuals; but not
only this, Ye were all of you called unto peace —
the Apostle says to the whole company of his
readers — in one body; that is, to the end that you

may become one body, or as connected with the
fact that you are members of one body. The end
and purpose of your Christian calling is this very
thing, to which you are urged. The foundation of
unity, on which the calling rests, is itself this very
thing. In either view or in both views, the common
call adds its emphasis to the individual call, and the
oneness of the life of all declares itself to be found
where, and only where, the personal life of each
abides. The Christian believer is one of a brotherhood. He cannot dwell apart in himself, or grow,
after the true manner, within the soul in separation from all others. He must ever be conscious, not only of a life-principle which he tries
always to strengthen in its power within his own
soul, but of a life-principle in which he shares with
his fellow-believers. The forces within them must
be the forces within him. The calling which comes
to him — and he must know this fact, if he would
know the truth and live as he ought — the calling
which comes to him from God is one that rests
upon his unity in life with others and moves towards
a harmony in life with them. The man is not called
alone as if to a solitude, but as one in a company —
as one who has a participation in the same inward
life-powers in which others of the company partici-
pate and one who is to have a community of life
with them. The brotherhood accordingly can never
be lost sight of, whether in his thought of himself
or of them — whether he is looking at the sources
and forces of his own Christian living or of theirs.
And the common principle, which at once rules in

him and goes forth in its influence from him to them,
must be this of which the Apostle speaks — namely,
ruling peace — for this is the one thing which unites
the brotherhood according to the Master's desire
and prayer.

The Apostle's exhortation therefore justifies itself
in every way as we look carefully into it. It lays
hold upon that which was a central force in Christ's
life, and which manifested itself most wonderfully in
the hours and days of His history when the greatest
of all demands and all necessities came upon Him.
It appeals to that which, in every individual soul
inspired by the inspiration of Christ's history, at
once reveals itself to be the power that brings the
life most happily and perfectly into harmony with
His. It presses with all emphasis upon the individual believer, and upon the company of believers,
the most impressive of reasons — those reasons
which are vitally connected with their calling to the
new kingdom, and their union with one another; —
and, by the energy which pertains to these reasons,
commends to thought and feeling the duty of which
it speaks. And throughout all the words which are
used, it keeps before the mind the example of
Christ and the gift of Christ — thus tenderly and
forcefully suggesting the imitation of the one and
the joyful reception of the other.

After our thought of all this, we cannot regard it
as strange that the words which the Apostle adds in
closing the verse, should be the words, Be ye thank-

ful — or, as in the strictness of their meaning they read, Become thankful, as with a new measure of gratitude, and an ever-increasing measure. It is as if, in his review of what he had said, he seemed to himself to have given his readers a beautiful vision of the peace of Christ, after the manner in which it enters, and may enter, into the Christian's soul; and of the same peace as, in its becoming a ruling power there, it may subdue all things to itself, and may bring the life into harmony and unity in all its development; and again of the same peace, as it may carry this harmony outward from the one soul to all souls, and establish the true unity among all; — and now, at the end, he finds but one feeling that can answer to the thought, and but one word appropriate for himself or for them. What could the word or the feeling be, but thankfulness — for the possibility and the reality of the vision.

And so the word comes down to us enriched, if we may say it, with the experience of the generations since the Apostle's day. We too may well move on to the realising of the vision, and to the joyful possession of the peace, with an ever-abounding gratitude to God.

THE LAW OF LIBERTY

If any man is a hearer of the word, and not a doer, he is like unto a man beholding his natural face in a mirror; for he beholdeth himself, and goeth away, and straightway forgetteth what manner of man he was. But he that looketh into the perfect law, the law of liberty, and so continueth, being not a hearer that forgetteth, but a doer that worketh, this man shall be blessed in his doing. — JAMES i. 23-25.

THE word of the Divine message, or what we often call the Gospel, is here presented to our minds as a rule of conduct and life. The writer takes up the thought of it, as we may say, at a later point of development, or from a different point of view, as compared with that which we discover many times in the Pauline epistles. To the Pauline mind the Gospel seems to manifest itself most readily as a system of forgiveness and justification. It opens the way by which the past can be set aside or remedied and the soul can escape from the burdens and dangers connected with it. It then bids the soul move on in its new course unfettered by the old sins and fears, and fills it with all hope and confidence as it trusts God lovingly for the future. But Paul himself, happily and peacefully as he turned his mind to this conception of the word, had another thought which dwelt upon it at a later stage

of its working. The new life was not only to begin,
but to go forward. It needed to go forward according to a law peculiar to itself — to move to an end
under the guidance of rules and principles of its
own. A system of forgiveness and a law of living —
these two elements pertain to the word, and must
pertain to it, if it is to accomplish the Divinely-
intended result. This writer, by reason of the special tendencies of his thinking and the natural
movement of his mind, looks most readily at the life
as developing, rather than beginning; in its growth
in the right way, rather than its moment of turning
from the wrong way. The rule of the true life, how
is it to be regarded and used — this is the question
which he would ask and answer. The special words
which he employs are impressively suggestive.

The word of the message, he says, is a law. To
his mind this expression naturally presented itself as
connected with his personal relation to the Mosaic
system. A strict observer of the duties imposed by
that system, he looked with deepest reverence upon
the law, which the Old Testament contained, as the
revelation of the Divine will respecting human living.
No new system introduced by God could have any
other end than this had had, or could be appropriately designated by any other name. But it is
interesting to notice that, when he assigns this name
to it, he adds a descriptive phrase having two parts.
He calls it the perfect law, and the law of liberty.
He had not been under the influence of the teaching
of Jesus, and of his thoughts concerning Him, with-

out seeing the differences between the new system
and the old. Stern moralist of the older type as he
was, he had learned long before the time of his
writing, even as Paul had, that there was something
of imperfection, with reference to *the working power
for the life of men*, in the law which, *as a revelation
of the Divine will*, was so clear and so full. The
study of his own life and of the lives of those about
him had made this imperfection continually more
evident. The perfect thing was to be waited for in
a development or manifestation beyond that of the
imperfect thing. The latter must give way to, and
pass into the former. The Gospel was to realise,
and had realised, what the law could not do. It
was to secure life in its completeness.

If we inquire after the elements which, being
added in the new system, justified this title of *perfect*, we may find them at two points. The word
which Jesus brought, opened on the one side, to His
disciples a wider and deeper view of the old law
than had been known before. They saw, under His
teaching, that there was no limitation in the demand
for human love, and service, and duty, to the boundaries of nations or of parties, but that everything
was wide-reaching as the world, and far-reaching as
the results of action could reach in the present and
the future. Life was no narrow thing. Individual
life was not confined within any limited circle of
surroundings. The law must become grander as
life became larger. The all-embracing character of
it, as it was now apprehended, changed its imperfection to perfectness, and the word of the new

message revealed this all-embracing character. They also saw, under His teaching, as a second thing, that the law penetrated, in a measure which they had not realised before, into the depths of the soul. The outward act was revealed to be far outside of, and distant from the source within, and that hidden source was the place to which the demand for right living directed itself. Life was discovered to be at the centre of the personality. It was found in the thoughts rather than the deeds; and the law was made to reach inward, as it was made to reach out-ward — into the inmost part of the man, as unto the widest limits of his relation to other men. The fact that the word moved thus inward made the law per-fect — making it deep in its reach even as life itself is deep. The perfection was revealed when the recesses of the life were opened. The new system did what the old had failed to accomplish.

But these elements — or rather this one element operating in two directions — were but secondary, as connected with the perfectness of the new system. The true and vital element was found in its central working-force. The word made love known as this force in the soul of the man, and as the source of what was given him in Christ. There was a weakness in the old law, which was fatal to its success, at just this point. Love was not manifestly at its centre. But the word of the message told the story of Jesus. It set forth His life as related to the law, and showed how He fulfilled its demands, as under the guidance of the great all-controlling principle. It declared His life also in its relation to men —

animated from its beginning to its ending by love to men and to all men. It made known how this love dwelt in His deepest soul — how it ruled and guided all things there — how it impelled all action from its most secret sources and purified the out-going life everywhere — how it took all demands and commands into itself and made the fulfilment of them beautiful service to God and to men, as that fulfilment realised itself in the sphere of the outward life. It did more even than this. It brought this love, so wonderfully manifested in Jesus' life, into the closest personal relation to each individual man to whom it addressed itself. It said to each one, This life, thus inspired and guided and governed, was lived in all its move-ment, and in the great things that it accom-plished, for you. You are what you are in the possibilities of your personal living, because it was thus lived. The future of good for you will rest upon it.

The word is a law, but it is a law with a working-force in it; a law, not imperfect because it cannot bring to pass the results it desires, but having with itself its own living power — the inspiration of love which moves the soul of him who receives it to do its bidding. Herein is the secret of its perfec-tion. The other elements already mentioned unite with this, as they deepen and widen the reach of the force which pertains to it. But they are second only, while it is first, because that which is the working-force, dwells not in them, but in it alone.

At this point we draw near to the other descriptive word which the writer uses — the law of liberty. The old system was ever liable to become for men a bondage, because it presented itself to them as a system of rules and commands. The inspiration of the obedience to it was not found within it. But when the new system founded itself on the love of God as manifested in Jesus, and made its appeal to that love in addressing each individual man, it made obedience a new thing. The love revealed stirred the love of the soul in return, and this love at once became the controlling power in the life. The result was what it always is when such an inspiration moves the man. Commands seem to lose their character as words of governmental authority. Rules are no longer thought of as limiting or fettering the life. The law is not a letter that kills, or a restraining force that awakens the opposition of the soul, or a thing which merely compels, by its threatening of penalty, a yielding to its requirement. Privilege takes the place of rules — the privilege of rendering service to another, who on his part has done everything for us. The man, with the new revelation in his soul, finds himself joyous in his doing of what he is asked to do, where he had been full of unwillingness, or rebellious as against superior power. The whole system under which he lives puts on a new appearance to his view. It is arranged in all its parts, and in its every demand upon him, for the best and truest development of his personal life. The rules are simply the method of growth formulated in words.

Obedience to them is the means of reaching the end. It is that by which the soul takes to itself the living forces and makes them effective. It is that which brings the imperfect, yet growing life into union with the perfect life — the life of man with the life of God, — and into such union that the one can be changed, steadily and rapidly, into the likeness of the other. The spirit which enters the man is no longer a spirit of bondage. It is a spirit of sonship. The whole relation is as of a son to a father — and this, not a father beset with the earthly weakness, who loses himself, ever and anon, in wilful assertion of his own will or in arbitrary exercise of authority, but a father, who realises in himself, and in his relation to his son, all the teachings of wisdom, and gentleness, and affection, which the long years give as they pass. The spirit of sonship is the spirit of freedom when the fatherhood is such as this, and when the sonship answers on its part to the fatherhood on its part. What is the law between the two? Surely it is the law of liberty. There is no bondage, and never has been since the two came to know and understand each other. The life is freedom, and the rule of the life is freedom's rule.

It was a great thing for one who had lived under the old system, and had been so strict an observer of it in its requirements as a legal system, to receive into his mind such a revelation as this. But the teaching of Jesus had made the light clear; and the darkness had passed away. The law meant liberty — not liberty without law or against law, but liberty working out the fulness of free and perfect life, in union with the Divine Father's life, through the law that is essential to its own develop- ment. This was the wonder and the glory of the Christian revelation. The rules of the Divine life in the soul of man were the rules pertaining to the orderly and natural movement of that life; and the natural movement is of necessity a free movement. But the free movement in this true life is inspired by love, and when this enters there is forgetfulness of all except its promptings. These promptings are to fulness of service, to largeness of obedience, to the fulfilment of every demand as in devotion to a friend and benefactor and father, to the giving of all to one who has given all, to the giving of the self to Him who has given Himself. The spirit of freedom, not of bondage, is the spirit of the Chris- tian system. Its law is the law of liberty — the law by which the son of the Divine Father freely guides his life and makes it like the Father's life.

The third expression which may arrest our atten- tion in the writer's verses is this: He that *looketh into* the perfect law, and so *continueth*. The word here used is a peculiar one which denotes a very intent and careful examination. The man is con- ceived of as looking thus intently into the Christian rule of life and conduct; and as doing so — not like the man who beholds his face in a mirror and passes on his way forgetful of what he is, but with continuous earnestness. Such looking the writer urges as essential. The necessity of it he appre-

ciated, as we may not doubt, because of the revelation of the new system, which he had received, as
a perfect law of liberty. Viewing the old law as it
was viewed in the earlier days, the man who would
conform his life to it must, as it would seem, have
looked into it with no passing or careless look.
It had rules for every day and every action, and
the man must know them and know whether he
was fully conforming to them, if he would discover
peace for himself. But here was a new system,
involving the freedom of sonship. Its animating
and governing principle was love. The love was
to be inspired by a love which had gone before
and given all blessing. This love-principle, having
its root and foundation in the Divine love, was to
penetrate every rule, impel every action, control
every feeling, stir the life in every part. It was to
be the working force that was always in operation.
It was to renew the man on all sides, and in every
department of his character and his soul. In the
system and its teachings the ideal of the life was
presented, and many rules and suggestions for its
realisation were set forth. The work of securing
for himself the realisation was left to the man.

What could be more essential to the end to be
attained than the one thing to which the writer
refers? Place yourself before the ideal life, and
think of your own relation to it. You must see it
not only once for yourself, and then move on your
way. You must look at it, not as a beautiful thing
apart from yourself, and after a little forget what it
is, and what you are. It is set before you as a

thing to be studied as you study nothing else. It
is a life, with its realities and its rules. It is a life
to be passed into your life through your turning
your life into its likeness. Its rules are to be followed, not in blind obedience, but in the freedom
of a love that is inspired by love. It is to be developed on every side, through all action and feeling,
from one day to another. It is to be brought to
its completeness through the union of your soul in
conscious fellowship with Christ who revealed the
ideal. No chance looking can give you the blessing. The man who beholds his natural face in a
mirror may go his way, and straightway forget
what manner of man he was, and no loss may be
suffered or growth of manhood be prevented. But
the beholding of the life for the soul is a different
matter, wherein the forgetfulness of the manner of
man that one is in comparison of the true soul-life
is fatal to the great result that is needed. The
thought must be ever on what the man is and on
what the ideal would make him, and so the look
must be continuously and intently on the word of
the Divine message which is the perfect law.

The writer now presents to us the *close relation*
between the looking into the law, after this manner,
and the doing of it. His words are striking words:
He that looketh into the perfect law and so continueth, *being* — as if, of necessity, in the very nature
of the case — not a *hearer* that forgetteth, but a
doer that worketh. The doing, as contrasted with
hearing and then forgetting, is assumed in the very

form of the sentence as essentially and vitally connected with the intent and continuous looking.
Christianity, in its teaching and its exhortations,
rests, and fitly may rest upon this assumption. It
knows full well that a man can hear its message of
life, or the proclamation of its demands, and can for
the moment even be impressed in his mind, and yet
can go away from the hearing with no abiding
thought of the deep significance of the word for
himself. He can forget what he has heard, and
forget what manner of man he is. The beholding
himself as in a mirror is a passing thing, and the
remembrance of it is lost.

But it knows also, and with equal assurance and
certainty, that if the man can be brought to study
the law of life — the law of liberty and love for the
free and freely developing life of loving service —
as he does who looks intently into some place where
there is hidden treasure, or some mystery whose
solution is of deepest import, the result will be and
must be the doing of what the law asks for. Intentness of looking indicates and proves earnestness
of purpose. When the intentness is in the sphere
of character, the earnestness naturally and even of
necessity moves into effort. The man is aroused
to action with reference to manhood. The knowledge of what manhood is impels at once to working
for it. Thoughtlessness makes forgetfulness. But
when the thoughtlessness has given way to thought,
and the chance looking to the continuous, serious,
earnest looking, a new spirit takes control. The
hearer becomes a doer; and the doer, a doer that

worketh to the attainment of an end which is deemed
vital to the soul. This is the way in which genuine
character grows and develops itself. It is so in every
department of our living. Awaken the man to the
intent contemplation of the ideal in any line, and to
the laws pertaining to it, and which it imposes, and
you have begun the work of the making of the
man — a work which will surely move onward
towards completeness, if the awakening is continuous. It is true, most of all, in the moral and spiritual sphere, for here is the essential life of the man.

It is to the end of the impression of the power of
this ideal on the soul, as we may believe, that Christianity, in its message, dwells so largely on the personality of Jesus, and stirs men by its every appeal to
look towards Him. To the same end it represents
His life everywhere, according to the reality of it,
as moving freely and lovingly under the perfect law
of liberty. Fix your thought upon Him, it says, as
a manly man studies and thinks upon the ideal set
before him. Place your life beside His in comparison with His. See there and then, with the seeing
of the inmost soul, what manner of man He was,
and what you ought to be and may be. Abide
there in the soul's thinking, as with the ever-continuing look of intentness. With this word, it almost leaves you to yourself for all the rest, for it
knows that, as you thus look, you will cease to be a
hearer only of the message, and will become a doer
of the law, fulfilling its requirements and carrying the results of your working into character. If
it can only move the soul by its appeal; if it can

lead it to put itself in the right place and the right attitude, it trusts the future with confidence.

And then it adds for the soul its final word, of assurance and promise: This man shall be blessed in his doing. The writer had learned, as he wrote these words, the deep thought of the Christian teaching. It is only when we stand apart with our souls unmoved by the contemplation of the ideal,— only when we are forgetful hearers, like the one who beholds his natural face in a mirror and loses all thought or care as to what he is, that the law of Christian living seems a law of bondage. It manifests itself thus to our vision simply because our souls are not stirred to activity for the soul's true well-being. But when we look into the law, and by looking intently see in it the law of liberty and of perfectness for the soul's life, and when our looking changes, as it were by a wonderful transformation, into doing and working, a new experience comes to us. It is *the experience* of the Christian's career. What is it? It is the experience not of hope merely, but of realisation. The blessing is not only a thing which we work for through the earthly course, patiently waiting for it, while we are ever attracted by the lovely vision of it as a future good. It is a present reality, known day by day, and in all the years, which abides in the doing, and pertains to it. The law of free service always has such blessing. Its demands come to us as calls upon our love for a loving friend. We answer them by our doing and working, as the sweet privilege of life. We grow in love, in beautiful character, in happy consciousness of right and blessed life, in assurance that the ideal is forming itself in our souls, in all that is most precious and delightful within ourselves, as we thus answer them. The inner life of the man becomes more and more a blessing to himself, and he moves on toward and into the future, knowing that greater and better things are awaiting him as he himself becomes better and greater.

The Christian teaching — the word of its message — the law of its free, happy, grand life, is a wonderful teaching and word and law. In the words of this writer the summons comes to you — and how reasonably and fitly — to look into it, and to make your lives conform to the ideal which it sets before you.

XVII

THE PASSING OF LIFE

For what is your life? It is even a vapour that appeareth for a little time, and then vanisheth away. — JAMES iv. 14.

I PLACE this question of the sacred writer at the beginning of what I would say at this time — having it in my thought to address my words to a company of educated young men in a university — not for the purpose of unfolding directly the answer which he gives to it, but rather because, in connection with that answer, it appears more indirectly, to offer the opportunity of gathering together a few thoughts upon the general subject of our passing life. The answer of the sacred writer, indeed, when regarded in itself, is one which almost from the necessity of the case loses its force in great measure to the thought of such a company. The shortness of the time appointed for us in this world is a subject which can scarcely make a very deep impression upon our minds when, in the fulness of youthful and manly vigour, we are just preparing for or commencing our work for ourselves. The way looks long before us, as we view it from the starting-point. How can we believe that we shall soon reach the end? We shall not reach the end soon. There are thirty or forty or fifty years before us, — and that

is not soon.. The man who has passed through
those fifty years may fitly say, if he will, that life
vanishes, for everything vanishes at last. But we
have not passed through them. We are at the
beginning, when all things are beautiful and hopeful.
God did not mean, surely, that we should call life a
vapour, and we cannot do so, at least till the realisation of the future has taught us the lesson which, as
yet, we do not more than half believe it has to
teach us.

Such, in substance, is what every young man says
to himself, and what the members of every company
of youthful friends say to each other, when their
thoughts are arrested for the moment by this question of life. The ending and the beginning do
not easily meet together. There are, however, some
things so closely connected with that constant passing away of the years which is to every reflecting
mind an appreciated fact, that we may urge them
upon those who look forward, as well as upon those
who look backward. If not all within the realm of
experience to-day, they are, at least, pressing upon
us from the immediate future, and must be allowed
their influence upon our minds even now, if we are
to guide our course by great principles or by the
great truths of our being.

Let me ask you, then, to call to your thought the
fact, that life is always passing out of the present into
the future. In one sense, life is wholly within the
present, for the future is uncertain, and the past is
gone from us. It is what we have and enjoy and

are, at this hour, that makes up our existence. We may have been anything in the time gone by, and it matters not, except as the results of that former time have worked out our present character and condition, or as memory has brought into the present the joy or sorrow which it then gathered into itself; while, as for to-morrow, it is an unknown season, which can never be ours until it is no longer to-morrow, but to-day. This is the view of life which lingers with us, in general, through all the earlier period of our career; and it is for us all one of the kindnesses of the Providential ordering, that the preparatory season does thus seem to limit itself to itself, so that no anxiety or fear mingles with the gladness of life's morning.

But this is not the truest view, nor is it the one which can abide the progress of time and the changes of the world. You come, my friend, to the hour when all the preparation is completed, — when the implements of your service have been given you, and you are bidden to go forth and do your appointed work; — and then, the present begins to seem to you almost as nothing. It is but a moment. It vanishes away into the future. You think of it only as it helps you onward towards that future, to which all your labours and hopes are pointing; in which your life centres and has its being.

And thus it will be, more and more, just according to the nobleness of your aims or the largeness of your desires and plans. While you see the days running by you with so little done, and yet the work opening more widely before you with so much to do — the attainments and progress already made appearing to your thought the smaller, just in proportion, perchance, as they appear to others, or even are in reality, the greater — you will be always pressing on, laying hold upon the things before, and finding yourself, in your dissatisfaction with the present, waiting most impatiently for that coming period which, in its turn, must lengthen and enlarge itself continually in order to fill the deep wants of your soul. The mind, in this way, alters its judgment of things completely as it comes to its mature reflection, and it is compelled to do so, because it sees that each to-day is only the time of fitting itself for each to-morrow, — the season of toil or warfare, while life passes out of this into the season of rest or victory.

But if all this is true, there is nothing necessarily of the brevity of life in it, nor is there anything which it is unnatural for us to think of when all is hopeful. There is, however, a suggestion that may have an all-important bearing upon our course of action in the world. Life is vanishing out of the present into the future now, and it always will be. What is the lesson? Is it not, that the future is the most certain and real part of our existence? Is it not, that the work of the soul for itself within the present is never accomplished, except as it takes hold upon the future and prepares for it? Surely, it would seem that this cannot be denied, for it is the very principle on which men are working everywhere around us — only that they limit their vision. You, my friend, for example, use all your energy willingly in your chosen life's work, with no thought of a full reward until perhaps the last ten years of the forty or fifty, to which you look forward, shall have begun; and if some one tells you that those years may never come, you give no heed to what he says — you do not even half believe in the possibility of its truth — because you know that your highest and best life is not here, but there. You are preparing for something in the distance before you, and you will not, for a moment, hinder your labours by admitting the thought that you may die before you reach it.

And as it seems to me, you are in one sense, perhaps in the highest sense, right in this. Your mistake is not so much in thinking that you have so many years awaiting you, as it is in thinking that you have so few. It is not so much in forgetting your liability to fall in death before the way is half-accomplished, as it is in suffering yourself to imagine that death, whenever it comes, is anything more than a point in your history — an event which changes, indeed, the sphere, but not the fact, nor the greatest wants, of your existence.

We grant you, then, the longest life — the whole of the half-century, even, that lies between you and the appointed boundary. We grant you that it is a long period, even as it seems to yourself. But that is not all the future, nor all your future. There are years beyond that. You are just as sure of sixty years or of a hundred, as you are of fifty; and you are absolutely certain of both. At some time within the hundred years, your sphere of activity will change. But that will not make the time that follows of less value to you — far from it. Rather, as to-morrow is more real and valuable than to-day, so the later period must ever rise to the rightly-thinking mind, into an importance which vastly outweighs the possibilities of the earlier one. This is the law of our being; a law which no reasonable man among us ever thinks of disregarding in his plan of living for this world, and a law which it is no more reasonable to disregard for any part of the future, so long as, whatever may be its dwelling-place, the soul remains itself.

I am speaking now, especially, of what you are doing for yourself, my friend. Why direct everything with so much care — why, as you are just passing forth into life, lay every plan, as you are doing, with so much thoughtfulness and so bright visions of hope, with reference to the ten or twenty years which shall close the next half-century of your existence, and then give not a moment's reflection, or the smallest part of your wisdom, to the ten or twenty years that begin the following half-century? And this is all the difference between the two periods, when we consider the subject as we ought. Life is not going to contradict itself, when you are sixty years of age. It is not going to bring in the fulness of success then, and so remain a harvest-time of joy for you until it suddenly ceases at seventy. No: — it will be passing out of the present into the future then, as truly and as constantly as it does now. Otherwise, it is nothing but a mockery. Otherwise, our largest desires and hopes and aspirations are to meet disappointment, and disappointment only. God cannot thus deceive the nature that He has Himself made.

The Gospel comes to us at this hour, then, and here is its first message: — Be ready, at every moment, for the future, and think of the remoter future, as well as the nearer one. It tells us also, that, in view of our present thought, death is nothing; — and as the man who labours with no care reaching beyond the night that closes these daylight hours is degrading his humanity to the level of the beasts that perish, so every one who limits his preparation for the future by the bounds of threescore years and ten, because, forsooth, the darkness of death is full of doubt or mystery, is forgetful of his soul's highest welfare and of the glorious birthright of his immortality.

Let me ask you to call to your thought, again, the fact that life is always passing out of the seen into the unseen. To the young child there is nothing, as it were, beyond what is seen. He lives among outward things, and fulfils the divine appointment in that he does do. But there is another destiny for those who have already begun the labours of their career in the world. They also are in the midst of outward things, but these are growing — gradually, it may be, but yet constantly — less and less to be their life. I do not mean that multitudes of persons may not go on from the commencement of their course to its close almost like children in this regard, or that multitudes more may not fail ever to look so earnestly at those things which in the Scriptures are called unseen, as to lay hold upon the eternal blessings. But I speak of the tendency — of the great fact alone, which is realised, in greater or less degree, in the experience of all thoughtful persons as they move onward in their course. The opening of mature years brings with it the necessity of working and the burden of responsibility. A man is obliged to force his way into the great company who are carrying forward the world's affairs, and to achieve for himself success in his chosen line. The carelessness of the past is over now, while the reality of the present and the future breaks in more and more impressively upon the soul. Now there is something in this very work of life which drives one in upon himself, to commune there with all that he knows of the spiritual world. Your work, my brother, does not merely go from yourself outward and thus terminate upon itself; but it returns from without inward also, so that you are growing up in your own inner life continually by means of all that you are doing. And to your serious thought, this will ever be the truest, greatest result of your working, so far as you are concerned in yourself alone. Yes, you may enter on your career with whatever plans you please — with all your efforts directed towards the attainment of reputation, or wealth, or any of the thousand objects of human desire that are at all worthy of an intelligent man, — and in the earnest pursuit of these, you may throw yourself purposely into the midst of external things, into the hurry and business of the world around you; but you cannot escape the ef-

fect of which I am speaking. There will be hours
— now and then at least, if not always — when you
will realise it. Life — whether we will it or not —
becomes sober. Life becomes thoughtful. Life, if
I may so say, becomes self-contemplative, very
rapidly, as we go on in it; and if you have any life
that is deserving of the name at all — so that you
are not a mere pleasure-hunter, or liver for the day
only — you will see that your work is most unreal
in itself, and most real in its influence within you.

But the time will only suffer me thus to hint at
this thought. It will impress itself more deeply
upon us when we think of the responsibility and
anxiety of life's work. The continual demand that
is made upon the soul for fortitude and energy — no
matter what may be the dangers, or disappointments,
or defeats, which are met with in the struggle of the
world — will force every man, even the strongest
hearted, to retire often and look after the sources of
new power. As such a man first becomes per-
suaded of his own weakness, indeed, he may begin
to search for these sources without himself, among
the fellow-workers around him. But the search will
soon cease; or, if it be resumed from time to time,
as the delusion of our life lingers with him, it will
show itself to be fruitless where the deepest wants
of the soul need to be supplied. No one human
mind can ever fully enter into the experience of
another, and the truth, that it cannot, men learn
more thoroughly as the years move forward. What
remains for the man then, but to go within himself?
And when he has gone within, what remains for him

there? Nothing, but either to strive to gather up his own energies anew, which have already failed him once, or many times, or to turn toward the powers of the spiritual realm. Let him, now, take whichever of these two courses he will, life has compelled him, in the hour of his greatest emergency, to abandon the external altogether. Life has passed, for that hour at least, from the seen to the unseen.

But with the earnest and thoughtful soul, which is faithful to itself, the effort will not always be — no, it will be less and less — to waken up its own un-aided strength, as its only resource. It will realise that its need is of a new power, higher than its own, and therefore it will try to hold communion with that which rules in the unseen world, and to search more deeply into the knowledge of that world, until it comes to feel and know that its own real existence is there. I do not say, let me repeat again, that all this is true, in its fulness, in the case of every mind. The blindness and sluggishness and passions of our humanity keep many from the truth forever. But I do say that such is the tendency — such is the les-son of the years — and you and I will be learning the lesson as we go forward towards the end, even though we may die, perchance, long before we have learned it thoroughly or received the richness of its Divine gift to the soul.

It is a universal fact, also, that we do not move far beyond the opening of mature life, before we are called to endure the separations and sorrows of this world. The joyousness with which even the lightest-hearted among you, my young friends, may

enter on the ten years immediately before you —
strong as you are in the confidence of warm friendships, and filled as you are with the bright vision of
the future — will find itself, surely it will, over-
clouded somewhat, before the ten years are ended.
It is better, no doubt, not to think about it much, as
yet. It will be time enough for that, when it comes.
But, even now, I ask you to bear it in mind that, when
it does come, you will know the fact within yourself.
If you are called, for example, a few years hence to
separate from one of your tried friends, as he is
summoned into the eternal world, you will find that
a part of your life is gone with him ; and, if you are
to each other what you think you are to-day, that
part of your life will never return from that world,
any more than he will. It will have passed, once for
all, from the seen to the unseen. Or if, in your personal experience, you find the struggle of the world,
even in its beginnings, harder for you than you had
pictured it in your happy dreamings, or bearing
with itself a suggestion, or perchance a threatening,
of possible failure as to your largest hopes, a similar
lesson will come to you — only it will be a lesson,
not from the region of the unseen into which another has entered, but from that unseen region
where the deepest thoughts and the central life of
your own manhood have their abiding-place.

But not only with sorrows or trials like these ; so
it is with every separation, with every disappointment, with everything that brings on darkness
instead of light. There is a sort of distinct and
independent life in these things, which runs on

parallel with our outward work. The world knows nothing of it. It is wholly of and within our souls, and it makes us leave the outward behind us, because it leaves the outward behind itself.

The very advancing years, also, tell the same story for themselves, because they are bearing us continually nearer to the unseen world. Life may not be brief to you now, because you have fifty years before you; but it will begin to grow briefer to your view after a little while, and just in proportion as it does so, will be the impressiveness of the thought that the unseen life is the real one. I do not ask you to realise this fully now — but the Gospel message to you, as you form your plans of living and go forth into the world, is: Do not deceive yourself with regard to the future: it no more constantly brings the unseen into the seen, than it bears the seen into the unseen.

In presenting the subject thus far, I have been led to allude to our active work in its bearing upon ourselves. Let me now ask you once more — my final thought — to call to your remembrance that, so far as our work in other respects is concerned, life is always passing out of *self* into *the world*. There is a deception which we all practise upon ourselves, in this regard. Not only at the outset of our career, but long afterward, we persuade our souls that the work which we have undertaken has a completeness in itself; and we press on with all earnestness, as if the whole of it centred in the few years of our sojourning on earth. But if our life is good for anything,—not given to mere personal enjoyment,—this is very far from being the fact. When we think of it rightly, you and I have not commenced anything, nor shall we finish anything. No, we simply take up an unfinished work, which some one else who went before us left for us to do and, after a season, we shall leave it, still unfinished, for some one else to take up anew, who shall follow after us. That is all.

I may draw an illustration from the place in which we are educated. The person who finds his appointed sphere for a life-work in a University may be said to have two great things — at least, among others — assigned to him to do : — namely, to maintain, in common with those around him, the life of the institution, and to make all possible progress in the department of learning to which he devotes himself. Now, in the former of these two things, he may find every day requiring new efforts or bringing new cares ; he may become absorbed in devotion to his work, and may go on with ever-increasing energy and enthusiasm to the latest hour. But, as he passes away from his individual earthly life, the life of the University moves steadily on beyond him. His work enters into its future, and mingles there with what went before and what follows after, until its relation to him may be altogether lost sight of, and forgotten. Thus it is, also, with the other portion of his duty, — even more clearly still, if that be possible. What has he done there, but advance his own science beyond the point where he received it, so that he opens to the future generation a wider vision and a larger field? So far from a completeness within his lifetime, it had its beginning centuries ago, perchance, and may endure for centuries upon centuries to come.

We, however, are but an example of mankind around us. The truth about our living is the truth about all living. The life of each individual may, in some sense, have a completeness; but surely it is not in its work. The work has no completeness. It has, in the light in which we view it at this moment, no meaning, except as it finds its way out of self into the world, and not only this, but into the world of the future.

The great law of self-sacrifice is dependent, in large measure, upon this fact. You cannot think rightly of the heroic sacrifices made in a great struggle for freedom, or in the work of a missionary to the heathen, or in any of the grander movements of the world in which those who have the most of life before them are called upon to give up that life most readily, except as you think of them thus. But when you thus think of them, the mystery is solved. The soldier may fall in his first battle, or the missionary in his first year of service, and yet not have thrown himself away for nothing. His life's work has ended just where it must have ended, had he been permitted to see the final success of his efforts. It has passed out of himself into the world.

And so everywhere, whether there be a voluntary offering like this or not. The friend beside you, whom you have known and loved with the ardour of a youthful affection, may pass away just as he sees the world opening before him and with the disappointment of every cherished hope, while you may linger on until the farthest limit of age is reached, realising all the visions that are now so beautiful to your soul. But your life — so widely different, as it seems, from his — is like his, in reality. You have gained nothing by your lengthened course, as we may almost say; for the question of sooner or later becomes an idle one, as you remember that the work of both takes hold upon the future, and abides there — as you remember that his work and yours may even unite together again, as they both move on beyond you into the coming age and form together, in some mysterious way, a portion of the world's inheritance.

The Gospel takes this closing thought, my friend, and says to you: Be as earnest and hopeful as you can be in all your work; but remember that it passes on in this world while you go to another, and that, when your earthly life has thus vanished away, you will remain.

But if this is so, here is one of the most vital and infinitely momentous truths of existence to all, and especially to those who are just forming their plans for the future. This thought may work backward in its influence, also, upon the two which have preceded it; for if your life is so passing away from yourself that what you are doing now finds its perfection only in later times, then the varied influences of your work in the unseen region of your soul are the only thing of importance connected with it, so far as *you alone* are concerned — and the growth of your character and interior being rises, of necessity, into the highest consequence. And again, if your work is leaving your hands as it were continually, and is to leave them altogether at death, to belong thereafter to the world only, not to you — then the years that follow the termination of your earthly course are worthy of your thought beyond all measure more than any of those which precede it, for then you are entering on a new stage of your existence, when all things may depend on what you are.

XVIII

THE THINGS THAT REMAIN

The things that remain. — REVELATION iii. 2.

THESE four words were written by the author
of the book from which they are taken
with a special reference to thoughts or visions
which were given to him. I venture to use them
simply for what they are in themselves. We
who belong to this peculiar community have
reached within these now passing days the last
brief section of our academic year. A large company included in our number have come not only
to the ending of this single year, but to the closing
period of all the years in which they can know this
place as the home of their united life. The final
hour lingers a little while, yet it so manifestly draws
near that it bears witness impressively of itself. It
comes, as it were, out of the distance and darkness
in which it has been so long hiding, and sends
forth, just before itself, its word of seriousness for
every one. While it lingers, the days have new
meaning and new thought in them. They are quiet
days, in the brightest and happiest part of the year.
But they are, because of their nearness to the end,
full of tenderness and suggestiveness, full of remembrance and of hope, full of earnest movement of the

258

soul, both inward and outward. They set the mind upon thinking in a way in which it has not thought before. They ask the man where he is, and what he is, in his inmost self; and, as they wait for his answer, they point forward.

It is to those especially, who are nearest to-day to the final ending of the pleasant life here, that I would say a few words appropriate to the hour and the season — words which will also have their application, though in less measure it may be, to all. The days, upon which these are now entering and which will so soon be past, may well suggest to them, I am sure, the thought of the things that remain. You stand to-day, my friends, at the last dividing-point of the course. Questions of your personal life must arise in your minds, at such a time. The questions above all others in which your manliest interest centres must be, What has passed away for us? — for each one of you, What has passed away for me, — and *What remains?* and the *second* of these two questions cannot but appear to your deepest thought the most vital one for yourselves.

The first thing that remains for you is the time before the end; which is indeed, very full of significance. In this matter there is found one of the marvellous kindnesses of God to us in this world — one of the proofs that He is a loving Father.

There seems to be so much time when we begin life, or when we begin anything that is of what we call long continuance, that we waste it as if it were valueless, or even misuse it to unworthy ends. The days and years pass on rapidly — flying by us, and beyond us, as if with wings; — but they come, as they go, and we think of the coming, not of the going. To-morrow will answer the purpose of to-day, and we may wait for it. Or it will, at least, give us the hours wherein the half-work of to-day may be made complete. We may, therefore, leave to-day's work half-accomplished. So we live on. We live as children, thoughtless of the present and trustful of the future. Or, with more heroic and manly spirit, we resolve, at the beginning, with a great resolve. The years shall realise wonderfully rich results for us in whatever we undertake. We will be more, and do more, than the idle multitude around us. We will be and do what is worthy of ourselves. But the resolution meets with weakness and hindrance as the time moves forward. The man's power is not what he thought it was. The end does not answer to the beginning. The hope changes to disappointment, and the years are gone. From whatever cause, when we come to a turning-point and look backward, we find that partial failure has befallen us. The past has not been what it might have been, or what we ourselves once hoped it would be when it came to its ending.

This is *our side* of the matter, and it is a hard thing for us all when we think of it soberly. Look at the subject for yourselves, my friends. You who are drawing near the end here at this time, cannot help thinking in these passing days. You who are closing the first year here, or the last, must find the impulse to reflection moving you because of this fact. Do you not discover for yourselves the common experience? The college life has not brought you all the results that you hoped for, or all that it might have brought. There is a loss out of the *plans* and *purpose* when the *achievement* is measured. The time has failed of its fruits — not all of them, indeed — life is not all waste or disappointment; but much of good is for every one, to-day, among, and only among, the things that might have been. It is not a pleasant thought to you or to me — this one of the failures; it is full of sadness. But it comes to us all in the quiet meditative days before the ending of the old years and the beginning of the new ones. This is *our side* of the matter.

But it is not the *Divine Father's* side. His thought, with which He comes to us as with inspiration and impulse, is, The quiet days are of the things that *yet remain.* They centre life in themselves. They have within them the time that is all-sufficient. Not all-sufficient indeed to do the work which might have filled the long years that are gone. They have not hours enough for this; and the work, if ever done, must wait for some new stage of life for its accomplishment. But all-sufficient for the *making of the man* with reference to the present and the future. The making of the man did not pass away, in its possibility, with the failure of the work. It did not require the years for its *beginning* and its *security*, though it did for its *early perfectness*.

Its beginning may come now; and as it comes, the truest life of the man will be secure. The *work* also will follow the *manhood* — not as easily, not as rapidly, not as perfectly as it might have done, had all been right from the outset; but it will follow beautifully notwithstanding. This is the Divine side of the matter. The thought is of present possibility, and thus of encouragement. The thought is of the days that remain, not of the days that are past. The thought is of promise and hope, not of hopeless loss; — and the summons which comes with the thought, is the summons to duty and manhood, in the time that remains, as *inspired* by the *promise*, and *cheered* by the *hope*. Let the deep sense of the past failure turn itself into a quickening power for the coming time, and let the man hear the *twofold voice* of the past and future as a *single call* to manhood.

The thought which has just been presented suggests easily, as a second thing that remains, the power of new resolve. This, in the movement of the soul, is the *starting-point* of manhood. The power lingers for all *with* the time, and gathers itself up in its full energy *within* the time. In the case of some men in every community, the newness of the resolve must be entire, if truest manhood is to follow. The old purpose has been wholly wrong; or the life thus far has been aimless, drifting along and away with the chances of the passing days. In a company such as that to which we belong, the latter experience is more often realised. There are persons here perchance, from time to time, who come hither, or abide in this place, with their will-power definitely and consciously set towards evil — the determination being, that the life shall be given to it. But if they ever appear among us, the blessing of the place is, that they appear as aliens to the commonwealth. Their soul-movement is not the soul-movement of the community. They belong elsewhere, and are not recognised as of the citizenship. Our oftentimes occurring experience, rather, is that we treat life as we treat the days. We enjoy it, as we enjoy them; but, as for the great purpose which is to govern it and truly create it, we defer this until the future, or form it only in some part of its force. This fault is not like the other. It is not the *man's* devotion of himself to wrong-doing with the *energy* of a *hardened nature;* but the *weakness* of *youth*, which fails to think of what is not within its immediate vision, and contents itself with what is thus near and around it. The weakness of youth, it is called. It is one, however, in which human experience shows that the youth is father of the man, for it tarries with the man — and with every man, in greater or less degree — long after the youthful years have passed. But it is one that tends to failure, and involves it.

The critical moment, however, comes by the Divine appointment. The day arrives, which is not the end itself, but which is near the end and testifies of it — the day which begins the brief closing season, and calls for and awakens thoughtfulness. What does it say to the thoughtful man, who now

hears its voice? It tells him that there remains
within the brief season one of the greatest of
gifts — the gift which may bear with it a remedy
for all weakness, and even for all wrong purpose,
in the past — *the power of a new resolve.* The man
may take the gift as it is offered to him, and, in the
yet lingering days, may make out of it a strong and
vigorous and glorified life; or, if it need be so, a
wholly renewed and transformed life, full of good
as the former one was of evil.

This is one of the ways in which we are educated
in this world. Something is always ending for us.
Something, as the ending time draws near, is ever
reminding us, as if by a friendly forewarning, of
that which is so soon to come. Something is whis-
pering in our ear, with the tenderness as of interest
in our well-being, that in the days between the forewarning and the ending, there is opportunity, and
more than this — a great force. Rise to the use
and exercise of the force, according to its true meaning. The power of new resolve stands ready to
change the character, or to strengthen it, if already
changed. Let it have its perfect work. So the
teaching comes, again and again, as we move on
from one period to another, — out of an old experience into a new one, — away from past thoughtlessness, or failure, toward the opening possibility of
the larger and better future. It comes with a peculiar impressiveness, when the premonition of the
end is given at the beginning of that brief closing
time after which youth in its fulness is to pass into
manhood, and the regrets for the old days mingle

with the hopes and fears for the new ones. The educating influence of such a time must tell upon the life which receives it, and the power of the new resolve must gain the mastery over the regrets and the fears alike, and must turn the hopes into assured confidence.

Closely connected with the matter of new resolve, though having an independence of it, is another thing which remains — the power of forming a new ideal. This is one of the best things which still linger with us in the closing days. And this, again, is a blessing for all. For the man who has had a low ideal, unworthy of himself, the possibility is of a wholly changed one, which shall elevate and ennoble him, lifting him by its grand force above his old self and bringing him into the realisation of what it reveals. But for men who have known something better than this — whose ideal has been, to their own thought, high perchance, and yet has not reached the loftiest limits — there is a great possibility. The ideal of life or manhood, in one sense, may never be higher for the true man than it is at the beginning. He may enter on his course with the thought of the perfection of himself as that at which he is to aim — and there can be nothing beyond this. We believe that there are many who have this thought in the early years, and who hold it fast in their minds and hearts. There are many such in our own number, as we would not doubt.

But what is the perfection of ourselves? It is a

happy thing that, as the years go on, this question
receives for us, and in us, a larger answer — more
full of meaning and richness. We do not stay, in
our thought, as we were in the earliest time. Our
thought widens and deepens. You do not wish, my
friend, — if you are in the right line of growth — to
be where you were a year ago, or ten years ago, in
the mind's life and the soul's life. You are more
than you were then, and you rejoice in the fact.
It will be so hereafter. You will be more ten years
hence, and thirty years hence, than you are now.
Youth in its fulness, just opening into manhood, is
a grand thing and a good thing — as beautiful as it
is hopeful, — but it is not everything, or the best
thing. The best thing is beyond it, in the distance.
And as for the progress of time which realises
what is better, and at last, away off beyond the
present vision, what is best — how much of its
rich gift is found in the enlarging and ennobling
of the ideal, which seemed to us, at the beginning,
as grand as it could be. The ideal has become
new to our thought — we discover in the after
days — because of the new meaning which it has
gathered into itself, and we dwell upon it with
ever increasing interest, as its influence within us
glorifies our souls. This is life as it was intended to
be of God, and as we know it for ourselves, in our
imperfect measure, in the growing years.

But here, as everywhere, life moves especially in
the critical seasons, and new revelations are made
to it as it turns from one stage of its progress
toward another. We gain, at the turning-points,

more than we do along the even pathway. Uplifting thoughts and larger views come to our minds
when the ending of one age arrives for us and
points onward to the beginning of another. The
thoughts then are suggestive and quickening for all
the future. The vision widens, and takes in, ever
afterward, more than it did before. We know, with
a deeper knowledge, by reason of these suggestive
thoughts and this wider vision, what is the meaning
and what is the reality of that ideal which we but
partially understood in the earlier time; and the
ideal of life seems, and in a certain real sense
is, a new one for us. Such is the gift which, as
the ending of one period of life waits a little for
the opening of the next one, remains within the
last days — waiting for us, each and every one,
to take it. It is one of the precious things that
remain.

And, in a peculiar sense and measure, does it
belong in the season just before the termination of
the youthful work for the educated man, for then the
taking into one's self the best thoughts for the future
is the most natural of all things. The season lingers
a little, we may almost say, for this purpose; and the
power of forming the new ideal is among its greatest blessings, — for, as this is filled out to greater
fulness at the starting-point of the manly years, the
life has its best and largest opportunity for development under its influence.

Allied to the influence of the new ideal is still
another of the things that remain. The power of

putting the life in the right path lingers with the
final days which turn the thought forward to the
future. And here we may speak of the matter
in two ways.

The life, what is it? · It is first, the life in itself —
the great, deep, central life of the soul, in which
the man is to live always. This may be put in the
right pathway in the season before the ending, if it
has never been set on that way before. The meaning and purpose of the season indeed, with all its
admonition of the future and tender suggestiveness
as to the present and the past, are found in its influence to this great end. There is no more earnest
call, in all the years, to any man in this company,
and no more loving one, than that which comes to
him who has thus far failed to be deeply thoughtful
of right living. He is called, in these passing weeks
before the ending of the days here, to do what has
not been done — to make the life what it ought to
be, by giving it a new beginning. And with the summons, comes the promise which rests upon the power
of forming new ideals and the power of new resolve
on the man's part, and upon the wonderful love of
the heavenly Father who sends the call and bids
the time yet linger. The blessing of all blessings,
in its possibility, is in the passing days.

But the life, we may ask again, what is it? It is
what pertains to its special work and duty. Here
also it may be put upon the right pathway. The
question of the particular line of life and service, is
a question which the young man just passing out
of the preparatory period most naturally presents

to himself. It is not essential, however, that he should answer it, at the moment. It may be that the time when the Divine wisdom would open the course clearly has not yet arrived. We may wait for the light until it is given us. But the *great principles* which should determine the answer and decision are needed *now*. Through them the life is to be set right, and when they have their abiding-place within the man, the answer in its more special bearing will be possible in its own season. The closing days wait for many with the gift of *this power* remaining within them. The man may establish in himself, with a strength unknown before and with a firmness such that it cannot be shaken, the principle that shall govern his choice — the principle which bears with it the resolve to do what the love of God and the love of man require of him. We do not go wrong, when this has dominion over our souls. Love shows the pathway, when the Divine moment comes for the particular decision. The days that wait may not be long enough for this decision, but they will be long enough for the entrance of the Divinely-given principle — and the life will be on the right pathway, so soon as this finds its legitimate place and force in the soul.

And now — with this power of new resolve, and of forming the new ideal, and of putting life on the right path, which is offered to all alike, and with this gift of the time yet lingering, in which each may take to himself the power — there is one

more thing that remains. It must be so, because
of the close relations of the company to one another.
The days that wait for us a little while before the
end carry in them *the power of gaining and of giving the best influence.* One of the marked peculiarities of the life which young men lead in a place
like this — in near and intimate companionship for
a term of years, having common pursuits, and
hopes, and impulses, and tastes, in large measure —
is this : that they may do much for the making of
one another, all along the course. Force for character, and for thought, and for feeling, passes and
repasses continually throughout the little community so thoroughly bound together. Consciously at
times, and far more often unconsciously, each one
gives to his fellow what is helpful in many ways —
and each receives as richly as he gives. When the
result is counted by the individual man, he finds
himself to be far different from what he was at the
beginning. New elements have come into him
which were unknown in the earlier time. New
force is manifested in his manhood. As he studies
himself carefully, and traces back to its sources
what he has gained, he discovers that he is partly
made, in the richest development of mind and soul,
out of the inward life of those whom he has known
so intimately, and with whom he has moved onward
in the journey of the passing years. He sees also,
as he studies the lives of those about him, that they
have, in like manner, received from himself. The
life of the united company has become quite another
thing than that which it was. The individuality of

each, indeed, has been preserved, but it has been enlarged, and manifolded in its powers and resources, and made more beautiful for the man himself and sweeter in its influence for other men, because it has taken into itself the best of that which came to it from every side. So it is always, when the individual life has suffered itself to grow, here, in the right way, and to become what the ideal of the place would make it. The man at the end, in this aspect of the matter, is created out of many men, and, in his turn, he has done his part in creating many men. It is a wonderful process and a wonderful result, but it is one of the interesting things of this our peculiar life, that we see the process ever going forward and the result ever coming nearer to its realisation.

But our thought now turns towards the closing days, just before the end and yet waiting for the end. In a singular measure and degree is the power of which we are speaking manifest in these days. There is something in the tenderness, and even sadness, of the ending time, which opens both mind and heart. No one has failed to know this, who has passed through the experience of this season in any of the years that reach far back to the beginning of the college history. Men get closer to each other as they draw near to the hour of separation, and the deeper manhood shows itself more easily. It opens itself both for the giving and receiving.

I have seen many times in life, as has every man who has moved along the years for a considerable distance, in which the opportunity for getting and for bestowing good seemed to gather itself up as it were, in a remarkable way, into a brief season. But I have never known a time when for manly influence on men a larger possibility offered itself, than in such days as these, through which those of you, my friends, for whom the past and the future are so near their dividing point, are now passing. A man among you need not even put himself to earnest effort to exert or receive the influence. He may simply open his soul and mind for its incoming and outgoing, and the result will be secured. Everything is helpful now toward good, if one only does not shut the door of his inmost self against it. But if with the serious life-purpose of a man who is just entering upon the needs, and the experiences, and the largeness of his manly years, he puts himself to the earnest effort, and determines to make for himself and take for himself what is in the closing time, he may find within it the richest gift of all the past to all the future. The thing that remains is the best thing, and it stands ready for each and every man, that he may receive it, in the brief season which is now beginning and is so soon to end, as a source of inspiration and impulse and life-giving force — a force and impulse and inspiration, which shall make the man ever larger in his manhood and happier also.

I think of human life — when it is lived after the right method and when the powers of mind and soul abide till the end — as always growing in the richness of its experiences and blessings, as it grows in

the forces and acquisitions, the knowledge and experience, that pertain to it. How can it seem
otherwise to us, when we view it as we ought?
But if so, may we not think of it, and must we not,
as finding in its closing season — after the admonition of the end has been given, but before the end
itself has come — a gift which will have a singular
blessing for us because, as it enters the life, it may
be taken onward into the greater world beyond?
And is not this gift, the power, realised in experience, of gathering up into the life all the elevating and enriching influence of the past years, and
the past associations, as it offers itself anew to the
mind and the heart? The evening time of the true
life will be light, by reason of the light of the by-
gone years thus shining out upon the coming and
eternal years.

So, in its measure, is it with the life of youth in a
place like this and surroundings like ours. The last
happy days are not happy only because of the
bright season of the year, or because the work is
mainly ended, or because there is promise in the
future. They are happy, far more truly and in far
higher degree, because in them is this thing still
remaining — that we gather up, as it were, in this
brief season all the possibilities of giving and of
getting, for the inmost soul of each and all, the influence for good of every individual life and of the
common life. The good which is thus offered, and
is thus made one's own, abides for the lifetime, and
beyond the lifetime in this world. It glorifies the
man, and makes the memory of the past years, and

the hopes and experiences of the future years, blessed as with a Divine blessing.

The days that are now passing by you, my young friends, who are drawing near the end of your course here, are full of meaning, of possibility, of gifts, whose value cannot be measured. Let me, as an older friend who passed through similar days a long time ago, ask you with all the emphasis of the subsequent years, to realise for yourselves their meaning, and take to yourselves the full measure of their gifts and their possibilities.

XIX

THE POWER OF PERSONAL LIFE

*Sorrowing most of all for the word which he had spoken,
that they should see his face no more.* — ACTS xx. 38.

THESE words are very human and very suggestive. We can easily picture to ourselves
the scene which the historian presents before us, as
he tells of the farewell which was given by the
Apostle to his friends. He had lived with them,
and among them, for the three preceding years.
During this period he had declared to them a new
doctrine, which had become life to their souls. He
had spoken the truth, as he believed it, with all
faithfulness and tenderness. He had warned them
of dangers, and assured them of consolation, and
borne witness to them of the purpose and plan of
God, and pointed them in all their needs to His
grace. He had given all to them and done all for
them freely, imposing himself in no way as a burden
upon them, but ever labouring for his own support,
that he might make all things that he did in their
behalf a gift. When the three years were drawing
near their end, he had been constrained to leave
their city, as violent excitement had been roused
against him and his teaching, and for a few months
he had returned to Corinth to renew his work and

strengthen the disciples there. The time for one
of the great annual feasts at Jerusalem was now
approaching, and he turned his course thitherward.
On the way, the vessel in which he was making his
voyage touched at a place in the neighbourhood of
the city where he had thus lived so long. The
opportunity was now afforded him of meeting once
more, for a brief hour, the chief members of the
church brotherhood which he had gathered together
by his preaching. He calls them to him and
addresses them in words of affection and retro-
spect; and as he thus speaks, he takes his final
leave of them, telling them of his belief that they
will never meet him again.

What a human scene it was — answering to the
experience of all ages, and bearing in itself the
evidence of the most natural sentiment, as we read
the words in which it is described. But of all the
words the most natural and most human are the
closing ones: They sorrowed most of all, because
they knew that they should see his face no more.

The picture, as we call it before our minds, is an
interesting one indeed, for it represents a thousand
other scenes in human experience as truly as that
which it offers to our view. But we would not
dwell upon it simply or mainly because of this fact.
The words, as we have said, are as suggestive
as they are human, and the teaching comes from
them — as it comes often from words and thoughts
— by reason of their suggestiveness.

Why was it that these Christian believers sorrowed

thus by reason of the thought that they should not see Paul's face again? It was because they realised at that moment, with an emphasis of reality, that the sight of the face was the sight of the man. If they could see him, they knew that there would rise before them the vivid representation of all that he had been and done, and of what he might do and be. They knew that the blessing of the past would have a new manifestation of itself, and the richness of the future would give a foreshadowing and fore-taste of its promise. It is always so, when we meet an old friend after a season of separation. His face bears testimony to us of all that is behind the pres-ent, and of all that is before it. The face, at such a moment, is the man. The loss of the face is, in a certain sense, the loss of the man. Everything passes into the sphere of memory, and the clearness and distinctness of the vision fade in some measure, and gradually, away.

But if the face is the man, it is *what the man was* that makes the renewed seeing of the face a matter of such strong desire. We do not care to meet again those who have left nothing of themselves within us, or for our lives, from the time of our last meeting. We bid them farewell without any stir-ring of sorrowful feeling. Let us look at the Apostle and his friends again. He had been for them a teacher. The message which he had brought to them was an announcement of something that they had not known or thought of before. As they received it and gave it its full power over their minds, it ennobled and glorified life for them. As a teacher, he had carefully explained to them what they were slow to learn. He had repeated and impressed his lessons. He had led them on from step to step, giving them new light when they were moving towards darkness. He had testified of what he believed, and had admonished and encouraged and inspired them, according to the necessity of their development in discipleship. He had been more even than their teacher; he had been, as he said to the members of another Christian brotherhood, their spiritual father. Their life had come from him, and had been watched over and cared for by him. Surely they might well, in view of all this, have grief of a peculiar sort in the thought that they were not to see his face again. How much would such a sight mean, if it could only be granted even for an hour! It would mean the fresh remembrance, with all its quickening and wonderful power for the soul, of the first beginning and the joyous progress in the early days, and the rich growth in the later time, of that new life for which they were thankful to God, and in which they were ever rejoicing as they looked onward and upward.

But there was something besides this, as the face represented the man. It was the personality of the teacher, and not only his teaching, which they called to mind as they thought of the separation. The teacher had, as we may say, *lived the teaching*, which he commended to their reception. He had given them deep thoughts, and sweet thoughts, and inspiring thoughts, respecting the great truth, as he had manifested before them its controlling power within himself. He had displayed to them in many ways, and on many sides, the greatness and grandness of human character as it is brought under the influence of the Gospel of God. How impressive must have been to their minds, at this hour of their last meeting, the words which he spoke in such simplicity and sincerity: After what manner I was with you all the time; how I shrank not from declaring unto you anything that was profitable; by the space of three years, I ceased not to admonish every one night and day with tears; in all things I gave you an example, that ye ought to help the weak: I hold not my life of any account, as dear unto myself, so that I may accomplish my course and the ministry which I received from the Lord Jesus. How the man must have risen before them in the magnificence of his Christian manhood, as these expressions came upon their hearing. And what a wonderful emphasis must have been added to them, as from the depths of a heroic soul, when, with the consciousness of what his life among them had been, he said: I coveted no man's silver, or gold, or apparel; ye yourselves know that these hands ministered to my necessities and to them that were with me; remember the words of the Lord Jesus, which I have remembered and followed, how he himself said, It is more blessed to give than to receive.

They must have taken knowledge of him — as they thus saw what was in his inmost soul — that he had indeed been with Jesus, and had learned of Him — learned of Him, not with the mind only, but in the life. All these words also, as they called up in review the years of their happy fellowship with him, must have brought to their recollection many others which he had spoken, and which had become life-developing for their own souls. Such words as he wrote afterwards have moved the life-powers for multitudes of the most intelligent and thoughtful men in all generations. They must have contained within themselves, in some peculiar sense and degree, the seed-principle of the true life for those who first heard, or first read them. To see again a man full of such thoughts would be a privilege indeed; to see him no more would be, as we may easily believe, a matter of sorrowful feeling, with which no other would seem worthy to be compared.

Let us now, as we think of the scene and its suggestions, ask, What are the thoughts which may fitly come to our minds respecting ourselves, and respecting life? The first, as it seems to me, is a thought bearing upon the matter of reward, and is this: —that the true and best reward of life, as it moves on its way, or as it ends, is not to be found in its success or its fame, but in that which Paul had here. Paul had done a remarkable work in this prominent city, and also elsewhere. He had become one of the great lights in the Christian Church, as it extended itself widely from its earliest home over the Gentile world. He had had wonderful success, as estimated by the possibilities of the sphere within which he put forth his efforts and to which he consecrated his powers. But what would his fame, or success, or prominence, or wide influence have been, if he had not been *in himself* what he was, — if the men who saw and heard him had not perceived within him the reality of that which he taught, — if, in a word, the man had not been more than the success or the fame, and had not been in the highest measure worthy to be seen again?

Men look forward with intensity of interest and desire to success in the attainment of reputation or power or position as an inestimable good in itself. They make the possession of this good the dream of their early ambition, the aim of their manly effort, the end of their living. When they strive or struggle for the prize, which they thus covet, in a selfish spirit, and with no thought or care for any service on behalf of the world, they persuade themselves that life has no nobler meaning in it, and is only intended to realise its gains. When they rise above this lower level, where they are unworthy of their manhood, and take into their thought and action what may be helpful to others, they think that the prize is glorified, indeed, by this motive which attends the effort for it, but that it is still in itself the same thing. In every way they press on after it, as if it were what makes life worth the living.

But a touching and beautiful scene like this, upon which we are dwelling in our thought for a few moments, has in itself another lesson and a widely different one. The grief, which was so manifestly and sincerely in the hearts of those about him, was more to the man who witnessed it than any success, in the outward measure of success, which he had had could ever be. It was so, because it bore testimony of the life which was in them, and of that which was in him. And so it is always. The earnest desire to see the face again — so that the knowledge that it cannot be is the most regretful of all things in the parting — shows that the associate of the years has much in himself, and has given forth much for us. A uniting force binds us together, and the life, which is now common to us both, owes its origin and its growth for ourselves, in greater or less degree, to what was, and is, in him.

I ask you to think of it, my friends — you who are soon to go forth from the pleasant associations of the four years in this place. What is the word which you desire most of all to hear from your intimate friends, and most of all to speak to them at the end? Is it not the word that carries in itself the hope of another meeting — the sight of the face, at some future time? Is not the hearing of this word, as it comes from the depths of the soul of the man whom you have known and loved, the reward of these years, beyond any other reward? And why is it thus? Is it not — when you have the thought resting upon the true foundation — because the word as it is spoken tells, with the emphasis of the soul's life, of what he knows that you have done for him by reason of what you have been in yourself? It is a testimony to what is more fundamental than success, and far nearer to the centre of life than fame. It speaks of what the man really is; and surely the manhood of the man is the highest reward of the years. It will be so, equally, in the coming time. Life is not going to turn around for you and become quite another thing, when the youthful season is past, from what it is now. There is a larger sphere before you, indeed; and there are greater prizes, as the world calls them, which are to be offered. But the human soul is the same, and the reward, which meets and satisfies the human soul in its inmost and noblest feeling, will be the same at the ending that it is at the opening of the manly career. This reward will be the testimony which comes from the living forces of other souls, as they have received the best of influence and inspiration from the man in whose behalf they testify.

The second thought, that comes to us from the scene to which we have turned our minds and its suggestions, as it seems to me, is this: — that the true standard for the measurement of value, as related to our personal lives, is not to be discovered in our teaching, or our working, but in our living. Paul's teaching was a marvellous teaching, surely; full of life-giving power, if any teaching could be. His working, in its constancy and its energy, and its wisdom in adapting itself to its purpose, was as remarkable as was the doctrine which he taught. But what a change there would have been in the manifestation before the world of both, if the man had not been what he was in his living. It was the man as formed under the influence of the doctrine, and putting forth the reality of himself into his work, that made the glory of his career. It was the man within him that made his friends grieve because they were to see him no more. So it is with us, each and every one.

The tendency of the world is to teaching and working. We become restless, with the thought that we are not fulfilling our mission among men, if we are not in action always, or ever declaring a message. But it is well for us to remember that, in the Divine ordering, a message of life is but half of itself, without life in the messenger, and that action, even when it moves in the right line, is a forceless thing, unless there is a vital energy behind it. Herein lies the effective power of enthusiasm. Enthusiasm means life in the man. He works, out of an inspiration which has become a part of his being, and so he moves victoriously towards results in other men. But in the moral sphere, especially, there is no true enthusiasm without life.

I ask you to look at your own experience, my friend, whether it be narrower or wider. Who is the man from whom the greatest power has come upon your personal manhood? Is it not the one whose inner life has been most rich and deep and true? Is it not the one from whom, whenever you have seen him — not only in the intercourse of every day, but even as he was passing along these paths and underneath these elms — you have felt that a lesson of genuine manliness has come to your soul? Such a man, if a teacher, has carried his moral and spiritual teaching for you in himself. It needed no word from his lips for your hearing, for you have seen it

284

in your seeing him. If he was a worker, even in the best lines of effort — even for the purifying and elevating of the souls of those around him — his real energy and force have been manifest to you as behind and beneath the work, and in the life. If he was a friend, you have known the influence, not simply when you have talked with him and have listened to the expression of his thoughts, but because you have beheld, in his whole exhibition of himself, what his thoughts have been to his own mind and for the development of character within himself. But if this be so, the very atmosphere of the place in which we are passing these years is full of testimony to the truth. No serious man, I am sure, can take his farewell of the place, and its associations, without giving to himself at least, if not to others, his witness, that the manhood in those whom he has esteemed and loved here as the worthiest men lies deeper than their doing, or their speaking, and that, in his desire to see them again, the chief impulse comes to him from what he knows them to be.

It must have been a delightful thing to the mind of Paul, that the men with whom he had lived for three years of intimate acquaintance wished so earnestly that they might have another meeting with him because he was what he was. But as he thought of their feeling with pleasure, he may well have said to himself, This wish of theirs is an evidence of the true estimate for myself, and for every other man. What we are is more than what we do. And so with us all. If we may have within ourselves the thought that the first of all things for the true life is

what we are, and that from this, as if its outgoing
and its fruit, is to go forth all that we do or teach,
we shall ever abide near the Divine ideal, and ever
be under its glorifying influence.

The third thought that comes to us from the
scene, which has been presented to our minds, and
its suggestions — and the last one to which I will
refer — is closely related to those which we have
been considering. It is this : — The true impulse of
the true man is, to develop rich thoughts within
himself, and to give them to others. A man does
not fulfil the ideal of his life any more truly than he
fulfils its obligations, if he simply performs the tasks
assigned him, or does his outward work, whatever it
may be. The mind and soul within him need to be
cultivated, and to be fruitful. He needs to have,
according to the possibilities which life opens to
him, elevating thoughts on the subjects which relate
to the highest interests of his manhood. It is such
thoughts, that enlarge and glorify his personality.
He needs them, also, for their helpful and upbuilding
influence as bearing upon those about him. If a
man lives for three years, as Paul did, in intimate
relations with a little community of men, or with a
few individual men, he fails of his highest duty, as
well as of his best influence, in case they are able
to gain nothing from the movement and working of
his inmost life. We were intended to do good to
one another in this way, as truly as in other ways,
and, if we have the vital power of the life in ourselves, we shall do so; for life always works from

the centre outwards and beyond itself. No man can take into himself the all-powerful, transforming Christian doctrine, and live with it as a vivifying force in his heart, without having much of its influence in the mind's thinking; — and if he has this influence in his thinking, it will go forth, often without an effort and almost before he is aware, to those with whom he is associated in the fellowships of the world.

The Christian man always has thoughts. He cannot be near to Christ, and dwell upon His love, without them. But the educated Christian has an especial duty and privilege in this regard. It is a part of his calling — as it is indeed, after his measure, in the case of every educated man — to be thoughtful. Education is not mere learning or the acquisition of knowledge — the accumulation of a treasure to be laid up in the mind, and to remain there without living energy. Education is the cultivation and development of thinking power, and a man who has not secured for himself this has, so far, wasted the years of his education. The knowledge and learning find their real end in this. But the highest moral and spiritual education is open to the Christian; and in this sphere, especially, is there no richest development without the stirring of the thinking power. A man must turn his mind in upon itself, and must study his soul, if he would set forward the true growth of his character.

What would Paul's life have been without his thoughts — where would have been the greatness of his character, which we now see so clearly, if there had been within him nothing of that inspiring Christian thinking which filled his letters with the expression of itself, and came with impelling power to the minds of those to whom he spoke? We need not look back to Paul, however. We may look again at ourselves. If we find, as we all do in the review of the years, that the growth of our individual lives in the mental and spiritual part is largely the result of what is given to us by the stimulating thought of others, the question is answered for us at once, and with emphasis. We miss half of the opportunity of life, we fail of half of its power for good, if we do not become thoughtful men — men who make the having and the giving forth of the most helpful, and the most inspiring, and the best thoughts the object of their constant mental effort. And how may this be accomplished better than in the way in which the Apostle realised it for himself — by putting the mind in daily communion with the highest truths of the soul's life, and bringing it to the continual, joyful study of the thought and inner life of Christ, the great teacher and the perfect man?

I have thus called your attention, my friends, to a verse from the sacred writings which tells of a parting between friends in the earliest days of the church. It has a fitness in its lesson for all of us in the closing of our academic year, and an especial fitness for some of us in the ending of all the academic years. The old scene in its great central feature, may seem to repeat itself, as the days pass on and the question of future meetings comes to those who must think of them with so much of interest. It is well for you to bear in mind the true standard of living, and the best reward of life, as you look back over the past and forward to the future. And it is fitting for you to remember that the thoughts for the inner life and the true life, which you gain and which you give, are the upbuilding forces for the souls of all alike.

That you may, every one of you, realise the blessing of giving and receiving, in all that makes life what it ought to be, is my best wish for you; and that you may know, by a constant experience, that it is more blessed to give than it is to receive, even as the Lord Jesus Himself said, is my largest hope; — the same wish and hope which I would have for myself.

XX

THE GIFTS AND LESSONS OF THE YEARS

*With long life will I satisfy him, and show him my salva-
tion. —* PSALM xci. 16.

I PROPOSE to suggest for consideration, at this
time, a few thoughts upon a somewhat uncom-
mon subject of discourse — the blessing of growing
older, or the increasing happiness of life as it advances. We hear much, in the ordinary conversation of mankind, of the brightness and joy of early
years. Almost every man looks back upon his
childhood with a sense of peculiar charm, and feels
that its half-remembered days were cloudless like a
summer morning, while the later years have been
clouded and darkened. The fond wishes of the soul,
therefore, return to that which is behind us, in the
nearer or remoter distance. We carry with us a
regret, which sometimes, indeed, hides itself away
from notice in the multitude of our employments, but
ever and anon breaks forth in its strength, that the
past cannot come back even for an hour, and that
we can never experience again what we once enjoyed. We listen also to much in the public dis-
coursing of the Church concerning the peculiar
privileges of the young and those who are just entering upon their career. They are believed to have,

not only the hope and promise of the world in themselves, but to be in a more desirable position than
older persons in what relates to their own individual
and interior life. How seldom, on the other hand,
are men of forty or sixty addressed, except to re-
mind them of increasing responsibilities, or, perchance, of wasted opportunities, or of the rapidity
with which life is passing, or the nearness of its ending. That a man is becoming happier as he is
getting older — that life is richer, and deeper, and
better for every right-minded person now, than it
was twenty years ago — seems to be a thought
which scarcely enters the ordinary mind, or, at least,
which scarcely ever so impresses itself as to demand
and find an utterance.

I believe that the truth is on the other side of this
matter, and I ask the kindly reader to follow me as
we consider the question whether it be not so.

In the first place, let us look at the happiness of
childhood or early youth, and inquire what it is.
It is the sense of life, in its beauty and joy, as a new
thing. It is freedom from anxieties, doubts and
fears. It is the calm confidence that there will be
provision for its wants. It is the affection of the
home circle, as yet unbroken by separation. It is
the awakening consciousness of the mind's own
powers and capacities, and the hope that, by means
of them, the man will in due time accomplish great
things in the world. We move onward a little way
beyond our first maturity, and we find all this
changed, in greater or less degree. The world seems

a different place from what it used to be, and we are roughly shaken out of our pleasant dreams and pict-urings. No wonder, that we begin at once to be dis-heartened, and to feel that the early years, as they ran away from us, bore with them beyond our sight the brightness and unalloyed happiness of life. Trials, and anxieties, and labours, and separations, and many failures in plans and purposes enter soon into the place of all that was so peaceful and beautiful. It is a world of hard work, instead of play. It is a world of sorrow, even, and constant disappointment. The golden period is behind us, not before us.

But stay a moment in your thought, my friend. Happiness is not freedom from care. We are reasoning and working beings — designed for ma-turity, and not for the mere beginnings. Thirty or forty years ago, perchance, you had not a thought going out beyond the enjoyment of the day, or the morrow, and therefore were free from care. But you were *doing* nothing; you were only, at the most, preparing to do. You had no true sense of your own capacities. You knew nothing of the sat-isfaction which comes from the full exercise of your powers, and from the accomplishment of real results. You were restless, even — just in proportion to the nobleness of your nature — to reach the hour when you might begin your portion of the world's work. If you are not in a morbid and diseased state of feeling for the time, you would not give up your present sense of manly force in action, and go back to the old condition, if you had the possibility, to-day, of choosing to do so once for all; — and you would

not, because you are assured in your deepest soul
that it is not only better, but happier, to be what
you now are, than what you then were. There is
no truth more certainly learned in a man's own
experience, than that, to the highest happiness of
our life in this world some element of conflict and
victory is essential. We must meet something of
opposition to try our powers, and must feel that we
have grown strong in overcoming it, or we do not
know one half of the glory of our manhood. And
this is the Divine appointment for mature and later
years. The child is a lovely object in his own place;
but he is only the beginning, the imperfect development, of that which is to grow to its perfection
afterwards. If the beginning were never to pass
into something higher, life would be a most unat-
tractive, because a most unfinished thing. The
work must be better than the preparation.

Look at your home life — where the happiness
of childhood seems to us often the only unalloyed
one, — and you will find, I am sure, that you are
mistaken here also. Love goes downward, rather
than upward. Your children do not, and cannot
love you as tenderly and beautifully as you love
them. The law of nature and the possibilities of
nature are only in the other way. You may turn
your thoughts backward to the home of your earliest
life and recall your affection for your father and
mother, and — pure as it may have been — it is not
what your affection now is for your own children.
You have entered upon a new stage of your being,
in this regard, and the feeling of to-day gives you

a deeper joy than the old one ever did, or ever could.

The delightful peace, that fills the home life and makes it such an emblem of heaven — my friend, in your childhood you *participated in it* only, but now, if it is in your home, you *make it;* you are the author of it, and give it its being. And it is more blessed to give than only to receive. I can think of nothing better, as related to this world alone, than to be the centre of happiness and affection for the inmost circle in which God has placed our lives and given us our sphere of highest duty — always bestowing upon others that for which their life is a continual, though it may be a silent, thanksgiving. But this the child cannot be, because of his position and his years. It is a blessing reserved for after life, and it makes the later years happier even than the best part of the earlier ones.

You were receptive, and wholly so once, in that former time, and therefore, again, you were free from many disturbing and harassing thoughts. Others cared for you, and you rested upon them. But now you are a giver in all things, and others rest upon you. You were made, however, to be a giver, and you have now only reached the fulness of your life. The labour, or fear of failure, or sense of uncertainty, which attends upon you as a condition of your giving, is all lost sight of when it is over, and the result is reached. It even passes into, and forms an element of the joy of the result — so that we enjoy the more what we do for those dependent on our care, the more of effort, and self-sacrifice even, our gift to them has made necessary. You did not leave your happiness behind you, and bid it a final farewell, when you first ceased to feel that your wants would be supplied by those on whom you used to rest. Far from it. You entered, rather, upon a new stage and measure of it at that very hour; and, if you will examine your own experience carefully, you will surely find that the new condition has been better than the old. Each of the two stages has been good in its own appropriate season; but the former one was only a mere preparation for the latter as that which is more perfect and more desirable.

But is not *the hope of great results*, which belongs to youth, you say, a more joyful thing than the *remembrance of half-results?* This latter, however, is the accompaniment of most lives in their middle and later portions. Life is all new and hopeful at the beginning; while, as we go onward, it becomes an old, familiar thing, known mainly by its imperfections. No doubt, I answer, we all lose much of the confidence of hope, after we begin to be actors in the world. We learn that we are accomplishing less — or in a different way, at least — than we used to think we should; and the work of reformation and good goes forward more slowly than it might. We are tempered, thus, and moderated in our expectations.

But if we are doing less than we anticipated once, we are *doing*, and not *hoping* only; — and, in so far as anything is daily done for the good cause in the world, the manly soul has a satisfaction in it which is deeper than it can have in its early hopes. It must be remembered, also, that, along with the moderating of our expectations as life advances, and keeping pace with it, there comes in the soul the growth of two feelings, which are all-important to its happiness in a world like ours : — the one, that the good cause, the cause of all good things, may go forward most successfully in a way other than that which we had thought of; and the other, the feeling of confidence in a wiser and higher power that is ever-ruling and overruling for its own best ends. The youth is confident, indeed, in his anticipations, and therefore he is happy. But he is strong in his own ideas and plans, and believes that all things must move after his own manner and through his own efforts. He opens the door, therefore, for disappointment so soon as he begins to turn his hopes into action. But the man, who has been working for a score or two of years, and has been a docile disciple in the world's school, has learned other lessons, which rob disappointment and even failure of much of their disheartening effect upon the mind. If life has wrought for him its legitimate result; if he has grown older in the way in which God would have him grow, he has become trustful in God's wisdom, and hopeful, in a less ardent way indeed, but in a more peaceful one.

And so, as I believe, the true effect of the progressing years is to bring us — even when we look at that which is brightest in the early part of life — to a happier, as well as a better state. But as we may fitly turn our thoughts, in our Christian meditation, rather towards what pertains to the soul and its relations to the future, I would more especially consider some other points in which life, as it would seem, must bring greater happiness to right-minded persons as they go forward in it.

Moving in this sphere of thought, I would say that as life, in any true view of it, is a plan of God, it must of necessity grow richer as it draws nearer to the end. I do not mean, of course, that it must be so in every man's actual experience. Some men, by their own choice and determination, put themselves in direct opposition to the Divine plan and working. They prevent the development of any good design in their existence, and we can expect nothing but perversion in their case. There are others, also, who, though they may have the hopes of the Gospel within them, become querulous, or dry, or hardened in their feeling, and thus lose out of their souls what is offered them so freely by the Divine favour. We can only speak on such a subject, however, of those who put themselves in the right line of living, and affirm what will be true of them, in so far as they do this.

But place yourself in the right position, and open yourself to the right influences — and you will not only know it must be so, but will realise for yourself that your life is a plan of God, and that He is carrying forward a work in you from its beginning to its consummation. How strange it would be, if there were no growth as the years advance, or if the growth were downward! Is it possible that, in His training of a soul for its immortal existence, what is best is placed at the very commencement, or that the progress of the plan towards its final issue can leave the soul less happy in the later, than in the earlier years? No — even those things of which we have already spoken are not, in this view of the subject, mere outward things or of the earthly life. In their influence, they belong to the character; and these things and all others, as they work in upon character, strengthen and purify and elevate it. They are designed to carry the soul forward in its own growth. They must make the soul happier than it was before it had known their power, and before it had grown wiser and stronger and better.

You may say that the carelessness, and the hopefulness, and the joyous outlook upon life in childhood, in themselves alone, are happier than what follows them and takes their place in maturer life — though, as I have already tried to show, I believe you are mistaken even in this view of them. But, when you look at your character, and at the plan of God in your own life, you cannot feel thus. This change indicates, and is, the progress of that plan. It was then near its beginning, but it is now, it may be, near its ending. What if, in this progress in your case, or in some cases, the outward man may, as the Apostle says, have been decaying — the inward man has been renewed more and more. Anxieties, cares, struggles, labours — the assumption of great responsibilities and the endurance of many hardships — have brought strength to you. They have awakened new earnestness, new confidence, new devotion, new love to men and to God; — and the work is drawing nearer to its completion.

The Christian man, and even, in his measure, the man who limits his view to this world and yet places himself in the line of life's best influences, cannot lose happiness as he goes forward. If he does, he is contradicting the Divine order and, therefore, is not in the true line of thought. As well might the victorious general rejoice at the beginning of the conflict, or at the first gathering of his forces, and lose heart and happiness in the moment of his approaching triumph. As well might we call the dimmest hopes joyful, and the full fruition sorrowful.

In every one of us who have been living in accordance with God's plan for these years past, and who do not shut our eyes to the consciousness of it, there is, and must be, a growing happiness as the plan works onward through the years towards its final result in a better life. If we do not daily enter into the experience of it, it is because we have become distrustful, or have clothed the past with an unreal beauty, or have allowed the fruits of evil habits to spread over our lives so widely that we cannot see the Divine working alone and in its own loveliness.

But there are some things wherein we grow naturally as the years advance, which tend directly to make us happier, as well as better men; and to two or three of these I would call your attention.

The man on whom the progress of life exerts its true

and legitimate influence comes into a kindlier and
more truly just judgment of those about him. The
tendency in early life — particularly, as we first begin
to associate with men — is to overestimate ourselves,
and underestimate them. We have grown up thus
far, as it were, within ourselves alone, and everything we therefore feel must be measured according
to our standard. The good that is in others, unless
indeed it may be those who are in full sympathy
with ourselves, we are often slow to appreciate, and
our judgments become severe. It is said that youth
is generous — and so it is, in some respects, far more
than the harder side of later life. But I cannot
doubt that the man who has gained anything of the
true spirit of Christ learns, under the natural influence of progressing years, to believe good of
others — that the familiar association with men, as
time passes on, brings us to see, in spite of all their
weaknesses or sins, the elements of good within them
and the possibilities of building up the nobler life.
If you, my friend, are becoming constantly more
distrustful of those around you; if your associates
and neighbours are judged more harshly than they
once were; you are, I am sure, not learning the true
lessons of the years, and are, so far at least, not
under the Divine guidance. But, on the other hand,
those who follow this guidance, and look through
their own weak souls upon the souls of those around
them, must continually grow more appreciative of
their better nature and more generously hopeful respecting them. And the kindlier you come to be in
your judgment of other men, the happier you will

be and must be; — and this is the true and un-perverted influence of advancing life.

The natural effect of the years in a really manly soul is, also, to make it softer and gentler in itself. I know that this may contradict the experience or observation of many persons. Habits strengthen, it is said, as life goes on, and we become harder and less open to impression. Not so, I believe, with those who are living nearest to the Divine method and are taking into themselves the proper influences of life. As I look back upon those of the genera-tion before me with whom I used to be most familiar, and who have finished their earthly course — strong and rigid and severe, as the men of that generation were, — I remember how the character softened into beauty, more and more, in the later years. If you also, on your part, will look upon those around you who are living rightly, you will see, I am sure, the gentler influences moving in upon their souls gradually and constantly as they move onward.

Life must bring us nearer to the Divine tender-ness and gentleness as we live longer under their wonderful power. But the years themselves have the same effect, in that they naturally wear away the rougher and harsher parts of the nature, and show how much mightier a power in the world gen-tleness is, than severity. As the gentler influences, however, bear sway more and more completely, the happiness of the soul becomes, of necessity, deeper and deeper — even as the beloved Disciple, passing out of that vehemence and energy which gave him, in his early manhood, the name of the Son of Thunder, came in the after period of his life into the quietness of the loving spirit which, as the old legends pictured it, faded away, without his dying, into the happiness of heaven.

My friends, I hope that you and I are growing gentler and kindlier as the years bear us onward. If we are not, we are losing one of the best, as well as one of the most natural influences of life, and are certainly not, in this regard, under the leading of the Divine Master. But, if we are thus growing, we know for ourselves, and in ourselves, that life is becoming happier as we are becoming older, far better than any one can tell us.

The right-thinking man, also, is naturally brought, as the years pass, to estimate more truly the comparative value of the things offered to him in this world. You know, my friend, with a deeper knowledge than you had five and twenty years ago, that the things relating to the inward life are better than those belonging to the outward; and if you are living in view of what you know, you are happier for knowing it. The experience of life has taught you that your success, or your wealth, or your fame, is not the highest of earth's gifts, — that these things are nothing in comparison with those which take hold upon the well-being of your inmost souls. In early years, we do not appreciate this, except as it is taught us by the testimony of others. Life is new to us in those years, and the outward things fill our field of vision. But the progress of time opens to us the truth, and experience impresses it more deeply upon the soul. Who can doubt that, as we learn this truth, we become happier? I do not believe that any man knows what rich and deep happiness is, until he has taken into the depths of his mind that which the lesson of the years teaches, and has made for himself the one great discovery, that it is what is internal, and not what is external to the soul, which fills the wants of our nature. We were created for the internal — for the development of *ourselves* to perfection; and it is here alone, that the highest joy can come.

We are thus led onward to our final thought: that, as the years advance, we are brought nearer to the heavenly life. There is a certain point in the history of all men who think at all — some time after early youth has passed away — when a great change comes over them. Every thoughtful man who is in middle life, or beyond that period, will recall it, I am sure, in his own review of past experience. I scarcely know how to describe it better than by saying, that we then began to feel, as we had never felt before, the significance of the fact that we are immortal beings. We had known this truth ever since we knew anything, perhaps, but we had not realised it in any impressive way for our thought. But now it becomes a vital thing to us, and we are never again what we had been. The idea of the eternal future, and of our life as passing into it — at any moment, it may be — cannot afterward be shaken off altogether from our minds. It

presents itself, whenever it will in our every undertaking, and may colour by its presence our entire
view of life.

A man may, indeed, resist the influence of this
thought so far that it will not regulate his subsequent course of action. In that case, it will only
disturb his quietness, from time to time, with its
suggestion of possibilities or dangers. But if he
gives it its proper force, and makes life to be what
it would dictate, it opens continually before him
the prospect of heaven, — not of heaven as a place
merely, or an outward reward, but of a beautiful
growth of the soul in all that is most desired and
desirable. The most elevating thoughts; the deepest emotions of love and kindliness; the nearest
communion with God which we ever have: — these
are the foretastes of the heaven which it opens to
us; a future life and time in which these shall become the permanent experience of the soul in a
place where all outward surroundings and all
friendly associations shall be adapted to the pure
inward and spiritual condition.

I cannot believe that life was intended by its
Divine author to grow less happy, as it should grow
older, *with such a prospect before it ;* or that it ever
does become so, except as we forget what we are
gaining from year to year — what we are passing
out of, and what we are passing into, as we draw
steadily nearer to the end.

It was not, then, without reason, that the Psalmist
sang of long life as a blessing, when it was lived in

the line of the Divine ordering. We may not forget indeed that, as the years go on, there are many things which try the soul to the very foundations of its being — toils, and burdens, and separations, and deaths of those we love. But in the wonderful working of all influences under the guidance of Him within whose plan are all our lives, even these things are made mysteriously to purify the soul, and thus, as it grows better, to make it grow happier also. So too, when the life reaches its end, and the deepening and increasing happiness of earth is exchanged for the greater blessedness beyond, the salvation which comes to the soul in its fulness is only that which had been shown or unfolded to it, in ever enlarging measures and clearer visions, while the years here were bearing it onward.

www.ingramcontent.com/pod-product-compliance
Lightning Source LLC
Chambersburg PA
CBHW060547030726
47498CB00005B/1302